The Crime
of Our Lives

Lawrence Block

by Lawrence Block

For
BARRY MALZBERG

The Crime
of Our Lives

Lawrence Block

A LAWRENCE BLOCK PRODUCTION

Before We Begin . . .

For over half a century—and, indeed, it's closer to sixty years than fifty—I've been spending much of my time and earning most of my sustenance writing crime fiction. Over the years I've had occasion to write some nonfiction as well, and a fair amount of it has been about the genre—about my experiences in it, and, rather more interestingly, about some of my fellow crime writers.

For the most part, I've avoided writing book reviews. In the early 1980s I did occasional reviewing for *Washington Post Book World*, and that was congenial enough (if spectacularly unremunerative) as long as the books sent to me were ones I liked. Two books that came my way, Thomas Perry's *Metzger's Dog* and William Murray's *Tip on a Dead Crab,* were just wonderful, and it was a pleasure to share my enthusiasm with the world, or at least that part of it exposed to the *Washington Post.*

But I found it agonizing when presented with something that didn't work for me. I knew very well what it takes to write a book, and didn't see it as a proper calling for me to fling mud at someone else's work. I remember trying to read one book, hating it, and realizing that that fault was not necessarily the author's. The right reader would very likely love the book, but I was not that reader, and it seemed only fair to return the book and let someone else review it.

Shortly thereafter I made it a policy to turn down reviewing assignments. I don't want to be in a position that compels me to either hide my feelings or say something uncomplimentary about a living writer.

When they're dead it's different. *De mortuis nihil nisi bonum?* No, screw that. The dead can stand a little criticism. One has to assume they're past caring. And if there is an afterlife, and some sensitive souls spend it paying attention to what's said about them back on earth? Well, you know what? They can go to hell.

In 1992, Richard Snow of American Heritage commissioned me to write an overview of American crime fiction. The result was "My Life in Crime," which the magazine published the following year. In it I discussed the field and my own experiences in it, leading up to a Top Ten list, which in fact ran to sixteen favorite writers.

I made sure all of them were safely dead. Not so that I could say bad things about them—I had only very nice things to say about them all—but because to include living writers was to invite the wrath of any friend I left off the list.

And, in fact, I generally try to avoid saying anything about a fellow writer so long as he has a pulse, and turn aside questions at public appearances.

The one exception I make is when I'm invited to write an introduction to another writer's work, or an appreciation for a magazine. I've done quite a few of those over the years, and here they are, collected for your perusal. For a while I contributed a column to Mystery Scene Magazine, which I called "The Murders in Memory Lane." It constituted personal recollections of a number of writers—all gone, alas, at the time of writing, and I miss them.

When I stopped writing the column, a few people asked me why. I told them I'd run out of dead friends.

Of course one never runs out of dead friends, because people keep on dying. Ed Hoch, Stuart Kaminsky, Joe Gores, Jerry Healy—I miss them, and regret their loss, but I don't seem to have a couple thousand words worth of reminiscence to share about them.

*　　　*　　　*

It's odd, this task at hand. An introduction to a book full of introductions, a reminiscence as prelude to a book of recollections. Sometimes over the years I've begun an introduction to someone's book of stories by advising the reader to skip my remarks and get on with the more rewarding business of reading the work itself. It's too late to do that now, isn't it? You've already suffered through them—unless you've somehow been prescient enough to skip these pages on your own.

Either way, we're through here, which is to say that it's time for us to get started. I've had the great good fortune to spend a lifetime in a richly engaging world, and I invite you to join me therein.

My Life in Crime

It was in the eleventh grade that I knew I would be a writer. The conviction grew out of two awarenesses that dawned at about the same time. I became aware of the world of realistic adult fiction, with all its power to inform and enchant and absorb one utterly. I became aware, too, of my own talent with words. I seemed to be capable of doing with them what I had been unable to do with a baseball bat or a hammer or a monkey wrench or a slide rule.

And so I wrote—poems, sketches, stories, the usual juvenilia. Artistically, my childhood had been one of deprivation, in that I was not the product of a dysfunctional family. Accordingly, the things I wrote derived less from experience and inner turmoil than from other writings that I admired.

During my freshman year at Antioch I sent what I wrote to various magazines, and they sent it back. I was not greatly dismayed. I mounted the rejection slips on the wall, displaying them like campaign ribbons. I suppose I was proud of them, and perhaps I was right to be. I was, after all, actively engaged in the process of becoming a writer, and they were evidence of that engagement.

I read all the time, and one of the many things I read, the summer after my first year at college, was *The Jungle Kids*, a paperback collection of short stories by Evan Hunter. A couple of years previously Hunter had hit the best-seller list with *The Blackboard Jungle*, and the stories were all about what were then called juvenile delinquents. (I don't know what you'd call them now. Kids, I guess.)

There were some fine stories in *The Jungle Kids*, including a positively Chekhovian tour de force called "The Last Spin," in which two rival gang leaders become friends in the course of a game of Russian roulette. There were other stories that were less remarkable, just good workmanlike efforts. But the book had a profound effect upon me because I found what Hunter had done at once estimable and attainable. I sensed that I could do what he had done here, and that it was worth the doing. I couldn't write these stories, but I could write stories that were good in the way in which these stories were good.

I sat down at once and tried writing a story about juvenile delinquents, and it was awful, and I left it unfinished. And then some months later I was living in New York and working in a publisher's mail room, and one Sunday afternoon I wrote a short story about a young man in New York who lived by his wits, making ends meet through petty theft and mail fraud. I didn't send it anywhere because I couldn't think where to send it, but eventually I recalled that Evan Hunter had published in a magazine called *Manhunt*, so I mailed my story off to it. The editor asked for a rewrite, complaining that my ending was inconclusive. I rewrote it and it came right back again, and the following summer, the summer of '57, I actually bought a copy of *Manhunt* and read everything in it and saw how to fix my story. I sent it off again, and damned if the magazine didn't buy it. Paid me a hundred bucks for it too.

And so my fate was sealed. For the past thirty-some years I've been writing crime fiction.

Imagine if my first sale had been to "Heloise's Household Hints" . . .

Poe started it. "The Murders in the Rue Morgue" is the first detective story, C. Auguste Dupin fiction's first detective. (He is a series detective too, reappearing in "The Mystery of Marie Roget" and "The Purloined Letter.") The story is a curious one, beginning with a couple of pages arguing the natural superiority of checkers to chess as a game of pure ratiocination and ending with an orangutan unmasked as the murderer. In its course its author set several remarkable precedents. He employed a mere mortal as narrator, a counterwheel to the brilliant detective; Conan Doyle took this device and made it his own, and ever since we have called such narrators Watsons. At the same time, Poe pitted his hero against the bumbling and unimaginative police, and this pattern of antagonism has characterized much of mystery fiction down through the years.

Both Nero Wolfe and Philip Marlowe are descendants of Dupin, so it is only fitting that American mystery fiction's highest accolade should be named for his creator. The Edgar Allan Poe awards are presented annually by the Mystery Writers of America in the form of a rather woebegone porcelain bust of the great man.

But did it really start with Poe? Men have been writing about crime ever since Cain invented fratricide, and I don't know that there is any level of literary excellence that some sort of crime fiction has not attained. *Hamlet* is many things, but if it is not a detective story, what on earth is? It is, to be sure, a story as vague and uncertain as its hero. Hamlet's father may or may not have been murdered, and Hamlet's mother and stepfather may or may not have done it. The plot of *Hamlet* has turned up, by coincidence or by design, in a number of mystery novels, not the least of them Fredric Brown's Edgar-winning first novel, *The Fabulous Clipjoint*.

Murder is a plot element in most Shakespearean tragedy, and many of the plays have their echoes in what we recognize as crime and mystery fiction, even as they have their antecedents in the playwright's own resource material. *Othello, King Lear, Macbeth, Julius Caesar*—crime stories, every one of them, their pages fairly dripping blood.

What is *Les Misérables* but a crime story? What is *Crime and Punishment* but a story of, well, crime and punishment? Or Dreiser's *An American Tragedy*? Or Hemingway's "The Killers"?

Still, it would seem that crime fiction does constitute a category, and that not every book with a crime central to its plot perforce belongs in that category. Certain novels are automatically shelved by booksellers and librarians as mysteries. Others are not. The

distinction is easier to make than to define; as Potter Stewart famously said of pornography, one can't define it, but knows it when
one sees it.

A few years ago the publishing industry had a very useful definition of a mystery. A mystery, everyone agreed, was any novel about a
crime that was sure to sell between three and six thousand hardcover copies. As a result of this perception, publishers with something
they thought might sell respectably did what they could to hide the
fact that the book was what most people would label a mystery.

All of this changed utterly, and a glance at the *New York Times*
best-seller list makes the reason clear. Week after week, books that
are undeniably mysteries occupy a dominant position. Writers like
Dick Francis and Tony Hillerman and Elmore Leonard and Sue
Grafton and Martin Cruz Smith and Robert B. Parker hit the list
with every book they write. Books about the detection of crime are
selling as well as anything can without promising weight loss and
personal growth.

Why?

The explanation that seems to me to make the most sense holds
that readers have a hunger for more substance than much contemporary mainstream fiction provides. Minimalist novels, academic
novels, novels that aren't about anything, tend to garner M.F.A. degrees and National Endowment for the Arts grants without winning
over the reading public. I read recently of a woman who has been
secretly getting her reading matter from the Young Adult section
because the books are about something. Much of crime fiction, too,
is about something. There's a crime, and there's an attempt to do
something about it. There are characters, and some of them live and
some of them die, and the whole thing works out in the end. Or it
doesn't, and that's how it works out. Either way there's a story, and
you want to know what happens next.

What happened next in my own career is that I kept at it. I
wrote more crime stories and sold some of them, to *Manhunt* and
other magazines. I wrote other stuff too. Articles for the male adventure magazines. A couple of true confession stories. A slew of

erotic paperback novels. The fabricated case histories of a nonexistent psychiatrist.

This and that.

The ideas that came to me and the stories that worked best for me tended to fit somewhere in the broad category of mystery and suspense. Even when they didn't start out that way, they tended to wind up there.

For example, in the late '60s I wrote a lighthearted little novel, a sort of *Lecher in the Rye* about a seventeen-year-old boy and his efforts to lose his virginity. Gold Medal published it as *No Score*, with the byline Chip Harrison, that being the name of the narrator. It sold particularly well, probably because it had a terrific cover, and I was moved to write a sequel, which the publisher imaginatively titled *Chip Harrison Scores Again*.

Well, I wanted to write more about Chip, but I sensed a problem. In the first book he'd been seventeen years old and innocent. In the second he was a year older and a good deal more experienced. At this rate he'd be a jaded roué in no time at all, and his charm was by no means the sort that age cannot wither, nor custom stale.

Inspiration struck. In the third book I put him to work for a private detective, a road-company Nero Wolfe, and knew he'd endure like an insect in amber. "You were wise to take this job," his employer told him. "Now you'll never grow old. You'll be the same age forever, like all the private eyes in fiction." He never did grow old, but not because of the mystery's fountain-of-youth properties. Alas, after he'd appeared in two Nero Wolfe pastiches I ran out of things for him to do and let him retire.

Some fictional detectives age. Some stay young (or middle-aged or old) forever. Some die. Agatha Christie left two manuscripts to be published posthumously; in them she killed off her two most enduring detectives, Hercule Poirot and Miss Marple. Nicholas Freeling did not wait for his own death to kill his Inspector Van der Valk. He bumped him off in midcareer in remarkably cavalier fashion, and alienated most of his readers in the process. Conan Doyle tried that, sending Sherlock Holmes over the Reichenbach Falls, but wound up bringing him back in response to popular demand.

At the other extreme some fictional detectives outlive their creators. A number of writers have kept Sherlock Holmes going, often matching him up with historical personages; in one of the more successful books, Holmes and Sigmund Freud wind up doing coke together. Robert Goldsborough wrote a Nero Wolfe novel after Rex Stout's death with the aim of amusing his mother. He has since written and published several more. A couple of years ago a dozen writers produced an anthology of new stories about Philip Marlowe, ostensibly to honor Raymond Chandler on his hundredth birthday. I suppose it's all right, so long as they only do it once every hundred years.

There are, as everyone knows, two kinds of people in the world: those who divide the world into two kinds of people and those who don't. The world of crime fiction gets similarly cleft in twain. Mysteries are divided into two categories: the tough, gritty, mean-streets, in-your-face kind, which is labeled hardboiled, and the gentle, effete, British country-house body-in-the-library sort, which is called cozy.

Stereotypically, the hardboiled mystery is American. It features, and is very likely narrated by, a private detective, a hard-drinking softhearted cynic who looks a little like Humphrey Bogart when he's not looking like Robert Mitchum. The hardboiled novel is written by a man and read by men. It is sour and downbeat and violent, and it means business.

In contrast, the cozy is English, written by women and for women. Its detective is apt to be an inspired amateur, male or female, and all its characters, except for the odd charming rustic, tend to be well spoken and courteous, decorous even in death. Its violence is offstage and unthreatening, leaning toward esoteric poisons and ingenious murder methods. The sleuth sets things right by working out an elaborate puzzle, and order is restored to a universe that is orderly at heart.

These stereotypes are undoubtedly useful, but they have their downside. Their rules are broken in book after book. British writers drag the reader through London's mean streets while Americans employ country-house settings. Women write hardboiled private-eye novels about tough female detectives, and other women read them, while men turn out intricately plotted cozies.

More to the point, the stereotypes tend to trivialize books of either persuasion. The cozy would seem to be frivolous, a bit of fluff that diminishes murder, and some of its specimens may have that effect. Yet no one epitomizes the cozy writer more than Agatha Christie, with her brilliantly worked plots and her comforting village settings. Her finest creation, Miss Jane Marple of St. Mary's Mead, is the ultimate amateur sleuth, a little old lady in plimsolls with a steel-trap mind. The books are entertainments, surely. And yet they are dead serious. Christie's concern in all her fiction, and especially in the Marple books, is the nature and origin of human evil. It is possible to read the novels attentively without becoming aware of it, but make no mistake about it, that is what they are about.

One of the abiding virtues of crime fiction, it seems to me, and one of the chief factors in its survival over the generations as a literary genre, is the seemingly infinite variety of work that falls within its scope. The house of mystery has many mansions, and it is a rare reader who can't find something he or she likes in one chamber or another. Now and then I run into someone who professes never to read mysteries, and I find such specimens at least as curious as those who read nothing else. The majority seem to be people who never got the knack of reading for diversion; a few are of the sort who read one mystery once, didn't much like it, and assumed all others to be the same.

As a reader I have always been able to find crime novels to read even as my own taste has changed and evolved. As a writer I have found that the genre's wide-spaced boundaries have allowed me to write whatever it has occurred to me to write without placing myself beyond the pale. Over the years I have written novels about four different series characters. Evan Tanner, who has appeared in seven books, is a sort of freelance adventurer whose sleep center was destroyed by a stray shard of shrapnel. He speaks innumerable languages, supports no end of lost causes (among them the restoration of the House of Stuart to the British throne), and slips himself and others across international borders, all in the interest of peace and freedom.

Bernie Rhodenbarr is a bookseller by day, a burglar by night. Typically he has to solve an intricate murder puzzle in order to extricate himself from suspicion incurred in the commission of a burglary. He is an urbane and literate chap, a nice guy who lives on the West Side and steals on the East Side. Whoopi Goldberg played him in the movie. (Don't ask.) His best friend is a lesbian poodle groomer.

Matthew Scudder is an alcoholic ex-cop, divorced, living alone in a cheap hotel in the West Fifties, eking out a living as an unlicensed private eye. He hangs out in churches (and, recently, at AA meetings in church basements), leads an angst-ridden life, and walks down some very mean streets indeed.

And I've already mentioned Chip Harrison, playing a horny adolescent Archie Goodwin to Leo Haig's version of Nero Wolfe.

Here's the point. These series differ considerably one from another—in type, in tone, in purpose. And I've also written a dozen or so non-series novels, and they don't run to type either. Yet all these books manage to be at home in the field of crime fiction. Not all my readers care for me in all my guises. One working private detective is a big Scudder fan but won't read my Bernie Rhodenbarr books, because he disapproves of my glorifying a character who is, when all is said and done, a miscreant and a lawbreaker. Some of Bernie's fans find Scudder's world too relentlessly downbeat for them. Quite a few readers have found Tanner's exploits too far-fetched to be taken seriously, yet others keep turning up to ask me when I'm going to write another book about him.

I should say something about fans. Compared with science fiction, mysteries barely have a true fandom. Science-fiction fans hold dozens of conventions annually, read everything written in their chosen field and nothing outside it, publish innumerable amateur magazines and newsletters ("fanzines"), and, according to one of the field's leading editors, are all fifteen-year-old boys who aren't very well socialized.

Mystery fans assemble at a single annual convention, the Bouchercon, named for the late Anthony Boucher, a mystery writer himself who was even more renowned as the field's foremost critic. Held every year in a different city, Bouchercon brings together upward of five hundred crime-fiction devotees. One writer is chosen as the annual guest of honor, his expenses paid by the host committee, but fifty or more other writers pay full price for the chance to natter away on celebrity panels, inscribe books for fans, hang out with booksellers and editors, and play poker until daybreak.

Bouchercon is always a great success, and a big factor here, I'm convinced, is the estimable nature of the people involved. Mystery readers are an uncommonly literate lot, inclined to choose substance over pretense every time. (It is interesting to note what they read outside the genre. Several mystery bookstores carry the odd nonmystery now and then because the proprietor just knows it will appeal to the store's customers. Most but by no means all of these books are about cats. W. R. Kinsella's *Shoeless Joe* sold well in mystery bookshops, as did Walter Tevis's wonderful novel of a girl chess prodigy, *The Queen's Gambit*.)

The mystery bookstore is largely a phenomenon of the last decade. Booksellers in general are a dedicated bunch, and the proprietors of stores dealing exclusively in mysteries would not be in the field if they did not love it. Their shops often have the ambience of clubhouses, and many of their customers drop in as much to chat as to buy books. Murder Ink, Grounds for Murder, Sherlock's Home, Rue Morgue, Footprints of a Gigantic Hound, Booked for Murder, Foul Play, The Butler Did it, Murder Undercover, Once Upon a Crime, Murder for Pleasure, Scene of the Crime—the ingenuity displayed in the stores' names suggests the resourcefulness of the people who operate them.

Finally, mystery writers themselves tend to be an amiable sort.

At a recent Bouchercon in Philadelphia, several of us were sitting around while one talked about his difficulties with an author. "What's remarkable about the guy," someone said, "is he's the only thoroughgoing S.O.B. in the field. I can think of a few guys I'm not crazy about, but he's the only real bastard around."

I could, if pressed, name another, but given the traditional nature of auctorial ego and artistic temperament, it seems extraordinary that such a large barrel should have so few sour apples in it.

While I'll leave it to psychiatry to explain why men and women who spend their lives writing about bloody murder should be so affable on their own time, I can guess why we're so apt to relish one another's company. The great majority of us are enthusiastic readers of crime fiction. Most of us were fans before we were writers, and continue to read one another's work avidly.

Besides such domestic organizations as Mystery Writers of America and Private Eye Writers of America, I belong to a fairly new outfit called the International Association of Crime Writers, with members on both sides of what we used to call the Iron Curtain. In the summer of 1988 I attended an IACW convocation at Gijón on Spain's northern coast. There were around sixty writers present from all over the world, and the majority of us were unfamiliar with one another's work. Most of our contingent spoke only English, and the group as a whole was a testament to the far-reaching effects of the Tower of Babel. There was one woman from Japan who came accompanied by an interpreter, and even he could barely understand her, as her first language was some outer-island dialect more exotic than Basque.

No matter. We all were crime writers. Everybody had a wonderful time.

Oh, all right. Enough stalling. A piece like this has to have a ten-best list, doesn't it? People do keep coming up with lists. An English mystery writer published a book not long ago with two-page discourses on each of his hundred favorites. (I'd mention his name, but he didn't mention mine, so to hell with him.) My list has a couple of special characteristics that ought to be pointed out. First of all, it consists solely of American writers. I am writing, after all, for a magazine devoted to matters American, so I trust I am not being excessively parochial in keeping foreign writers off this particular list.

It is perhaps largely for this reason that most of the writers I've listed are of the hardboiled school. Born in the detective pulps after the turn of the present century, hardboiled crime fiction was very much an American invention.

After Poe, pre-eminence in the mystery field passed to the British. Wilkie Collins wrote *The Moonstone*, Sir Arthur Conan Doyle created Sherlock Holmes, R. Austin Freeman wrote about Dr. Thorndyke, and any number of British writers went on to develop the detective story as a suspenseful adventure, an intellectual exercise, and a look into the darker corners of the human psyche.

Some American writers followed in these British footsteps, with greater or lesser success. But in the pulp magazines another tradition was born. Crude, violent, rough-edged, cynical, often antiauthoritarian, pulp crime fiction spoke in a new voice that caught much of the spirit of post-World War I America.

A group of writers centered on *Black Mask* magazine forged hardboiled fiction into something honest and vigorous; of their number, Hammett and Chandler emerged to produce something that will pass for Art. Years after their passing we still write this sort of book better than anyone else. The French have an insatiable appetite for the roman noir and accord the work considerable critical respect—rather more, I sometimes think, than it truly deserves. But very few of the hardboiled crime novels published in France are homegrown.

The British can write hardboiled books, but some of their best tough writers set their books in America, as if to say that a hardboiled crime story demands an American setting. James Hadley Chase and Peter Chambers, the latter a devoted admirer of Raymond Chandler, are quite popular at home but have never traveled well, and few of their books are published here. Their American settings and dialogue may strike a British reader as perfectly authentic, but they clang horribly on an American ear. (This sort of thing works both ways. An American woman writes British cozies set in England, to the rich delight of an enormous American following. Most of her fans assume she's English, a mistake no English reader would be likely to make. "She gets everything all wrong," an English fan told me. "I can't believe your lot takes her seriously.")

At the same time, I have to admit that the preponderance of the hardboiled on my list reflects a prejudice of the author. I tend to prefer hardboiled (or, if you will, realistic) crime fiction and to see it as of more fundamental importance than softer, gentler books.

The reader will further note that my list has no women on it. This would certainly appear evidence of blatant sexism, and perhaps it is. In rebuttal I would argue that Agatha Christie and Dorothy Sayers would certainly be on my list but for the fact that they are British. And several American mystery writers would be on the list, too, but for the happy fact that they are alive.

Because, you see, I have listed only writers who have gone to that great Bouchercon in the sky. I have mentioned how generous and amiable mystery writers are, how much I enjoy their company, how well we all get along. If you think I am going to change all that by assembling a list of favorites and leaving some of them off it, you're out of your mind.

One last note. This is a list not of best books but of favorite writers, although I have occasionally mentioned a book or two that I remember with special fondness.

Here's the good news: Instead of ten favorites, I seem to have come up with sixteen. And it was easy to put them in order. I just used the alphabet.

Anthony Boucher (1911-68)

Boucher's reputation rests largely upon his influence as a reviewer, which was monumental. From 1951 until his death he wrote the weekly "Criminals at Large" column for *The New York Times Book Review*, covering virtually everything of note published in the mystery field. He reviewed paperback originals at a time when no one else took much notice of them, discovered and encouraged promising new writers, and widened the tastes of his readers while sharpening their perceptions. During many of the same years he also reviewed plays and opera and science fiction, appeared on radio and television, edited a science-fiction magazine and a number of anthologies, and died young after many years of intermittent ill health.

In addition, he wrote eight novels and a couple of dozen short stories. I think it is safe to say that he would have been more prominent as a writer of fiction if less of his energy had gone into other pursuits. His books are slight, but their charm and the skill with which they were written keep them sprightly and engaging. My own favorite, though but dimly recalled, is *Nine Times Nine*, a locked-room mystery investigated by Sister Ursula of the Order of Martha of Bethany. (As a reviewer and editor Anthony Boucher was always an easy mark for a story with a nun or a cat in it.)

It was published under the name H. H. Holmes, an alias previously employed by a mass murderer of the nineteenth century. "Anthony Boucher" was itself a pen name; the author's actual name was William Anthony Parker White.

Fredric Brown (1906-72)

I discovered Fredric Brown around the time I began selling stories to the crime pulps, and I read everything of his I could get my hands on. One time, after a hard week at a literary agency where I was gainlessly employed as a reader of unsolicited submissions, I read *Murder Can Be Fun*, in which a murder is committed early on in full view of dozens of bystanders—by a killer dressed up as Santa

Claus. I had a bottle of bourbon on the table, and every time Brown's hero took a drink, I had a snort myself. This is a hazardous undertaking when in the company of Brown's characters and, I've been given to understand, would have been just as dangerous around the author himself. By the time the book was finished, so was I.

Brown was a playful, inventive, prolific writer who never wrote the same book twice. *The Fabulous Clipjoint*, his Edgar-winning first novel, is perhaps his best book. In it young Ed Hunter joins forces with his uncle Ambrose, a former carnival performer, to investigate the murder of Ed's father. The Chicago background is perfect, the carny lore a big plus. *The Screaming Mimi* and *Night of the Jabberwock* are also vintage Brown. My own favorite is *The Wench Is Dead*, about a sociology professor immersing himself in L.A.'s Skid Row in the name of research.

James M. Cain (1892-1977)

While he is generally regarded as one of the seminal figures of hardboiled crime fiction, Cain would have no part of it. "I belong to no school, hardboiled or otherwise," he insisted.

Oh, well. The writer is always the last to know. On the basis of two books, *The Postman Always Rings Twice* and *Double Indemnity*, Cain's place in the field is assured. He wrote sparely and convincingly of ordinary and fundamentally decent human beings moved by sexual passion to commit murder for gain. A whole generation of strong American fiction, the archetypal gold-medal novels of Charles Williams and Gil Brewer and others, springs directly from these two books.

Not everyone admired him. "Everything he touches smells like a billy goat," Raymond Chandler complained. "He is every kind of writer I detest, a *faux naïf*, a Proust in greasy overalls, a dirty little boy with a piece of chalk and a board fence and nobody looking."

Hey, don't hold back, Ray. Tell us what you really think.

I always think of Cain when the subject of film adaptation comes up. Several of his novels were filmed, and he was often asked how he felt about what Hollywood had done to his books. "But they have done nothing to my books," he would reply. "They are right over there on the shelf, exactly as I wrote them."

Raymond Chandler (1888-1959)

Chandler has long been the intellectual's darling, a mystery writer for people who don't like mysteries. On the one hand, he talked of taking murder out of the English drawing room and putting it in the streets where it belonged. At the same time, his characters spent a surprising amount of time in the homes and haunts of the California rich, a West Coast equivalent of the country house on the moors. His achievement, it seems to me, is less that he brought the traditional mystery into the alleys and gutters than that he put a novelist's spin on the pulp tradition of *Dime Detective* and *Black Mask*.

All the novels are first-rate, except for *Playback*, a tired and confused effort published a year before the author's death. I suppose my own favorite is *The Long Goodbye*, which shows rather more of Chandler's detective Philip Marlowe than did any of the previous books. In its exploration of Marlowe's friendship with Terry Lennox, the book is as much a novel of character as of plot. If ultimately flawed, *The Long Goodbye* thereby fits Randall Jarrell's definition of a novel—a lengthy prose narrative that's got something wrong with it.

Stanley Ellin (1916-86)

Stanley Ellin was a perfectionist, working slowly and deliberately, producing a page of typescript on a good day. He admitted to having rewritten the opening paragraph of a short story as many as forty times before going on to the next paragraph and polishing each subsequent page in similar fashion before proceeding further.

It is possible to write short stories in this fashion, and Ellin consistently wrote the best mystery short stories of his time. His very first published story, "The Specialty of the House," endures as a classic, although it is probably less surprising to today's reader simply because so much fuss has been made about it. But all of Ellin's stories are wonderful. He managed only one a year, sent each in turn to *Ellery Queen's Mystery Magazine*, and never had one rejected.

He received more financial remuneration, if less critical acclaim, for his novels. (He did not write them as slowly and laboriously as the stories. You can't.) An early private-eye novel, *The Eighth Circle*, impressed me when I read it years ago. His later novels never worked terribly well for me, but the short stories are timeless, and a national treasure.

Erle Stanley Gardner (1889-1970)

Eighty-two novels about Perry Mason. Nine about D.A. Doug Selby. Twenty-nine (under the name A. A. Fair) about the private-eye team of Donald Lam and Bertha Cool. If Stanley Ellin crept through his stories at a snail's pace, Erle Stanley Gardner wrote like a man with his hair on fire.

I discovered Perry Mason when I was twelve, and I don't know how many of the books I read over the next three or four years. They were relentlessly formulaic, and in a sense, if you'd read one, you'd read them all. On the other hand, if you enjoyed one, you would enjoy them all.

The prose narration was sloppy, the descriptions clichéd. Gardner hurried through those parts, and so does the reader. But the dialogue, effortless for the author, was absolutely masterly, and the courtroom scenes, however unrealistic they may have been, worked magically upon the page.

Mason himself changed over the years. In the earlier books he himself was a shady character, willing to bend and even break the law in the service of a client. He grew respectable in his middle years, when most of his cases were serialized in *The Saturday Evening Post*, and he turned staid and dull later on.

After a period of neglect Perry Mason seems to be coming back into favor with readers. Try one of the pre-war Masons—*The Case of the Sulky Girl* is a good one—or any of the A. A. Fair books. The latter are very different, breezily narrated by Donald Lam, and characterized by much better writing than the Masons.

Dashiell Hammett (1894-1961)

Hammett's colossal reputation rests upon a very small body of work. After several years laboring for the pulps, he published five novels in as many years, then wrote virtually nothing for the remaining twenty-seven years of his life. And the last of the novels, *The Thin Man*, is really not much good.

No matter. The others are superb, as impressive now as when they were written more than a half-century ago.

Hammett was a Pinkerton detective before he started writing, and his experience informs his work. But his greatness is far more than a matter of being able to write knowledgeably of crime and criminals. Both his literary style and his artistic vision cast an unsparing light on Prohibition-era America. In sentences that were flat and uninflected and remarkably nonjudgmental, he did much the same thing Hemingway did. I would argue that he did it better.

The Maltese Falcon is my own favorite, and the Bogart film won't spoil it for you; the book quite literally is the John Huston screenplay.

Chester Himes (1909-84)

If Hammett brought the special perceptions of a detective to crime fiction, Chester Himes came at it from the other side. He began writing toward the end of a seven-year stretch in an Ohio state penitentiary. His first books were novels of the black experience, critically successful but not widely read. In 1957 he wrote his first crime novel and introduced his pair of Harlem detectives, Grave Digger Jones and Coffin Ed Johnson, who were to appear in eight more books.

Savage, violent, and wildly funny, Himes was never as successful in America as he was in France, where he lived from 1953 until his death. I don't know how well the books hold up, but I know they were terrific when I read them, especially *Cotton Comes to Harlem*.

John D. MacDonald (1916-1986)

The creator of Travis McGee, boat bum and self-styled salvage expert, had an M.B.A. degree from Harvard Business School. I don't suppose that's anywhere near as weird as Wallace Stevens working for an insurance company and writing Peter Quince at the Clavier in his spare time, but it's a far cry from the way Hammett and Himes prepped for their writing careers.

It seems likely that McGee, hero of twenty-two fast-paced novels, will stand as MacDonald's greatest creation. By the time McGee made his initial appearance in *The Deep Blue Goodbye* in 1964, MacDonald had already published some forty books, all but a handful of them paperback originals. They're almost all crime novels, and they're almost all excellent.

The French, connoisseurs of our literary dark side, don't know from MacDonald, and on reflection I can understand why. For all the ecological foreboding of the McGee books, MacDonald's vision is not on the surface noir at all. His sensibilities were always Middle American, and his characters approached difficult situations with the problem-solver attitude of an engineer. But there is a darkness to MacDonald, evident in his unparalleled ability to limn a sociopath, present too in that neglected late work *One More Sunday*. It is not the knee-jerk darkness of the noir world view but the somehow bleaker darkness of a light that has failed.

Some of the late McGees are weak books, but so what? Start with *The Deep Blue Goodbye* and read them all in order. Of the non-McGees, I have especially fond recollections of *The End of the Night* and *One Monday We Killed Them All*. Each in its own quiet way is dark enough to make noir look like a light show.

Ross Macdonald (1915-83)

Ross Macdonald was born Kenneth Millar and wrote his first mystery novels under that name. Then he wrote one book as John Macdonald and five as John Ross Macdonald, finally dropping the "John" to avoid confusion with John D. MacDonald.

He began writing in frank imitation of Hammett and Chandler, and the early books in the Lew Archer series are markedly Chandleresque, with Archer wisecracking briskly in the Philip Marlowe mode.

With *The Doomsters* in 1958 and *The Galton Case* a year later, Macdonald came into his own and went on to write a series of books unlike anything before him. Against the background of the Southern California ecosystem in metastasis, Archer bears witness as the mills of God relentlessly exact retribution for long-past sins.

A few years ago my wife and I were in West Africa for three weeks. We had plenty of luxuries, like food and water, but nothing to read, and the only books and magazines available were in French. Then, in our hotel in Lomé, the capital of Togo, I discovered five Lew Archers, second-hand paperbacks that had been badly printed in India. The newsdealer wanted an extortionary ten dollars apiece for them, and I paid it willingly. They sustained us all the way back to JFK.

Of course we had read them all before, some of them two or three times. It didn't matter. It is one of the singular properties of Ross Macdonald's fiction that ten minutes after you have turned the last page, every detail of the plot vanishes forever from your mind. I'm sure I could reread those five books right now without much more than the faintest sense of déjà vu.

In a sense the plot of every book is much the same. A character did something reprehensible twenty or thirty or forty years ago—in the war, perhaps, or in Canada. Now things begin to fall apart, and, even as Archer rushes around trying to forestall disaster, the guilty and innocent alike are sucked down into the primordial Freudian ooze.

Wonderful books. Read any of the post-1958 Archers for a start. And don't throw it away when you're done. In a few years you'll be able to read it again for the first time.

Ellery Queen
(Frederic Dannay, 1905-82, and
Manfred B. Lee, 1905-71)

Prohibition must have been a time of great self-discovery. Even as Americans were discovering themselves as hard and tough and cynical, and confirming this discovery in the works of Hammett and Chandler, so were many of us waking up to find ourselves clever, and rejoicing in our mental agility by working crossword puzzles, playing contract bridge, and repeating the Round Table talk of the Algonquin crowd. And by reading intricate deductive mystery novels and trying to figure them out.

The books of Frederic Dannay and Manfred Lee, two cousins from Brooklyn, were bylined Ellery Queen and featured a detective of the same name. (They were not first-person narratives, however; Ellery Queen wrote about himself in the third person.) They took the intellectual puzzle of S. S. Van Dine's insufferable Philo Vance and elevated it to its highest level. Vintage Ellery Queen mysteries (*The Greek Coffin Mystery, The Chinese Orange Mystery*) feature a formal challenge to the reader at the point where all the clues needed to solve the puzzle have been furnished. The books were always fair, and diabolically clever.

During the '40s Ellery Queen matured artistically, and the books became more than brainteasers, with a richness of character and setting and mood. *Calamity Town, Ten Days' Wonder,* and *Cat of Many Tails* are especially successful.

The books alone make up a towering body of work. Add in a slew of first-rate short stories, innumerable radio plays, and four decades at the editorship of the field's pre-eminent magazine, and the extent of Lee and Dannay's achievement begins to become clear.

Jack Ritchie (1922-83)

For years I did the same thing whenever I got hold of a copy of *Ellery Queen's* or *Alfred Hitchcock's Mystery Magazine*. I looked to see if there was a story by Jack Ritchie. If there was, I read it right away.

Ritchie was a miniaturist in an age when writers are judged by the number of trees cut down to print their work. He wrote only short stories, and he tried to do so without wasting a word. His work was sprightly and surprising and always engaging, and he never wrote an awkward sentence or a lifeless line of dialogue.

Then one day he died, and his stories went on appearing for several months and then trickled out, and ever since I have picked up those magazines with diminishing anticipation. Nowadays I look to see if they've reprinted one of his stories. If they have, I read it right away.

Rex Stout (1886-1975)

I know several men and women who are forever rereading the Nero Wolfe books. They read other things as well, of course, but every month or two they have another go at one of Stout's novels. Since there are forty books, it takes them four or five years to get through the cycle, at which time they can start in again at the beginning. They do this not for the plots, which are serviceable, or for the suspense, which is minimal even on first reading. Nor are they hoping for fresh insight into the human condition. No, they reread the books for the same reason so many of us do, for the joy of spending a few hours in the most congenial household in American letters, the brownstone on West Thirty-fifth Street that is home to Nero Wolfe and Archie Goodwin.

The relationship of these two, Wolfe the genius and Archie the man of action, is endlessly fascinating. Ultimately it is less Wolfe's eccentricities—the orchids, the agoraphobia, the food and drink, the yellow pajamas—than the nuances of character that keep us transfixed. Stout wrote these books almost effortlessly, in a matter of weeks, and his first drafts went to the printer with no need to change so much as a comma. They seem as flawless today, and utterly timeless.

Jim Thompson (1906-76)

Thompson published twenty-nine books during his lifetime, all but one of them paperback originals. More than half of his output appeared in the '50s, with five books each published in 1953 and 1954. Most of them were published by Lion Books, a third-rate house. They were rarely reviewed and never commanded a wide readership. In the late '60s Thompson did a few novelizations of films and television shows to make ends meet. By the time he died, all his books were long out of print.

Now, seventeen years after his death, Jim Thompson is the hottest writer around. His novels of doomed losers and flippant sociopaths are all back in print, and there are several films in production or recently released, among them the highly successful *The Grifters*, the screenplay of which earned the mystery writer Donald E. Westlake an Oscar nomination.

For years Thompson was unjustly neglected. Now I suspect he's getting rather more attention than he deserves. His books are intermittently wonderful, casting a cold eye indeed on life and death and providing an utterly unsparing view of the human condition. They are also intermittently awful, flawed by chapters of slapdash writing, adolescent character development, and mechanical plotting.

The Killer Inside Me, Pop. 1280, and *The Getaway* show Thompson at his best. He is surely an important writer and very much worth reading, but it helps to keep it in mind that the stuff ain't Shakespeare.

Charles Willeford (1919-88)

In one of his Hoke Mosely mysteries, Charles Willeford supplied a character who had retired after a lifetime spent painting pinstripes on the sides of automobiles. He now lived in a development in South Florida where he liked to walk through his neighborhood with a kind word and a cheerful smile for everyone he met. He carried a walking stick, its hollow interior stocked with poisoned meat pellets; the affable old boy delighted in poisoning every dog that crossed his path.

I can't think of anyone else who could have created that little man, let alone made him work. Willeford kept coming up with quirky characters and put them in wonderfully quirky books. A career soldier in the horse cavalry and a highly decorated tank commander in World War II, he wrote a variety of books over the years, all of them providing a skewed vision of the universe.

It was in the Hoke Mosely novels, starting with *Miami Blues*, that Willeford came into his full powers as a writer. He wrote four of them, each better than the last, and was just beginning to win the wide readership and critical recognition he deserved when he went and died. It was the sort of joke he would have appreciated.

I am told he left the rough first draft of a fifth Mosely novel, darker than dark, unpublishably dark, with Hoke rounding things out by murdering his own teen-age daughters. If that manuscript's out there somewhere, I want to read it. Meanwhile, read the other four in order. Willeford wrote two volumes of autobiography, *I Was Looking for a Street* and *Something About a Soldier*. Both are a treat.

Cornell Woolrich (1903-68)

A couple of years ago I read a Woolrich short story in which a pulp writer locks himself in a hotel room and works all night to meet a deadline. When he's done, he falls asleep, exhausted; when he wakes up, he's horrified to discover that the pages are blank. There was no ribbon in the typewriter. Presumably the hero took each page in turn from the typewriter without noting the absence of words on it.

Cornell Woolrich was capable of this sort of plotting. Loose ends and illogical twists and turns abound in his books, but they don't really matter. His great strength, it seems to me, lay in his unrivaled ability to make novels of the stuff of nightmares. Woolrich's characters prowl tacky dance halls and alleyways. They smoke dope in strange apartments, swallow spiked cocktails, and run hallucinating through unfamiliar streets. The suspense is relentless, the sense of impending doom ever present.

Woolrich wrote his best books early on, starting with *The Bride Wore Black* in 1940.

*　　*　　*

The most noteworthy aspect of my list, it seems to me, is the number of significant writers I've had to leave out. I could easily have included a dozen more. If I were fool enough to include living writers, I'd have had to write a book. Because, for all the talk one hears of the mystery's vintage years, I think it is abundantly clear that the very best crime fiction ever is being written today. These are the good old days, and a very real reason for the huge popularity of mysteries is that the genre is in its Golden Age. Many of the very best writers alive are writing crime novels, and they are doing extraordinary things within the genre, things no one has previously attempted.

If there's a lot of wheat, surely there's no end of chaff. I suppose 90 percent of what's being published today is nothing special, but when was it ever otherwise? The good stuff, I assure you, is very good indeed.

You'll excuse me, I hope, if I decline to point it out to you. But think of the fun you'll have digging it out for yourself!

Edward Anderson

An introduction to a 1986 edition of Thieves Like Us:

There is a scene in *Bonnie and Clyde* that lingers in the mind. The two bank robbers are holed up in a tourist cabin. They are in bed together, aglow in the aftermath of lovemaking. As Bonnie Parker, Faye Dunaway had tended to romanticize the two of them, seeing them as Robin Hood types and as star-crossed lovers. "If we had it to do all over again," she asks, "would you do anything differently?"

Warren Beatty's Clyde Barrow considers the matter. "I'd do a lot of things differently," he tells her. And he goes on to explain that, for one thing, he'd never rob banks in the same state where they lived.

While he is telling her this, we see Dunaway's face. And for an instant she registers the recognition that this guy is, when all is said and done, just a *zhlub*, and the two of them are not indeed a road company Romeo and Juliet, and that if this turkey had it to do all over again, he'd *do* it all over again. There is that instant, and then she pushes all this new knowledge out of her mind and they are together again.

In *Thieves Like Us*, the lovers have few illusions. Bowie and Keechie never assume heroic proportions in their own or each other's eyes. Bowie treasures her because she is a "little soldier," what a more urban crowd would call a stand-up broad. She, having made her choice, elects to stand by her man. She thinks they ought to be able to hole up in the hills forever, and he has fantasies about retiring to Mexico, but they both know what we know—that there is only one way out of this maze.

Thieves Like Us was published in 1937, at a time when bank robbery was an attractive profession in the American Midwest. The automobile had given thieves a technological advantage with which the law had not yet caught up. With the Dust Bowl reeling under the Depression and the country closer to some form of class revolution than it has ever been before or since, the bank robber attained instant celebrity; if he was not necessarily idolized as a hero, he was at least perceived as an ordinary Joe trying to make a living.

Edward Anderson captures wonderfully the ordinary quality of criminals. Bowie and T-Dub and Chickamaw are neither the exploited downtrodden souls of typical proletarian novels of the period or the warped misfits of more psychoanalytically oriented fiction. Crime is how they make money, and they make as lot of it quite easily. (T-Dub and Chickamaw can't hold onto theirs. Bowie can, but gets little joy out of it.) They see themselves as working men whose work is robbery, and see everyone in the straight world—lawyers, politicians, businessmen, Wall Street capitalists—as "thieves like us."

One suspects Edward Anderson knew the folks he wrote about. Born in Texas in 1906, he grew up there and in Oklahoma, where he worked on newspapers. Between jobs as a reporter he shipped out on a freighter, boxed, and played the trombone. He tried fiction, and after a few sales to sports and adventure pulps, he spent three years riding the rails, hoboing across America in the early years of the Depression.

In 1934 he was off the road, married in New Orleans, and writing fiction again. The following year his first novel, *Hungry Men,* won a *Story* magazine prize and was published. An engrossing and marvelously authentic novel of men on the bum, it derived directly from Anderson's own experiences.

Before he wrote *Hungry Men,* Anderson wrote about criminals for the true-crime magazines. He made fictional characters of them in *Thieves Like Us,* and the book was very well received, with at least one critic grouping him with Hemingway and Faulkner. His career could hardly have looked more promising, and there seemed little danger that the man would run out of things to write about, or that readers would tire of prose and dialogue that was as flat as the prairie and as clear as the open sky.

Astonishingly, *Thieves Like Us* was Anderson's last published fiction. He went out to Hollywood, worked for a couple of the studios, but didn't like it. (What a surprise!) He returned to journalism, worked in California and Texas, and ultimately edited a paper in Harlingen, Texas. He wrote more fiction but never sought to publish it, lived to be sixty-three years old, and died essentially forgotten by the world of literature.

We always wonder why a writer stops writing. I sometimes think we should marvel more at those who *don't* stop. In Edward Anderson's case, one wishes for an explanation, and asks in vain; one might as well seek to know why Bowie robs banks, or why Keechie stays with him.

Still, that doesn't stop me from wondering. And I wonder, too, what those stories were that Edward Anderson wrote but never published. Did he destroy them? Were they consigned to a bonfire after his death? Or are they even now reposing in some attic in East Texas, waiting for someone to discover them?

Time will tell. For now, Edward Anderson has left us two small masterpieces which, half a century later, have not a single false word between them. And that's not bad for a country boy.

Fredric Brown

An introduction to Dennis McMillan's small-press edition of
The Case of the Dancing Sandwiches, *1985:*

The question was straightforward enough. Would I care to write an introduction to an unfinished and previously unpublished Fredric Brown novel? My answer came without hesitation. Of course, I said. I'd be delighted.

Doubt came later. What, I wondered, could I possibly find to say? I'm by no means an expert on the life or work of Fredric Brown. Since I first discovered him in the mid-1950s, I believe I've read everything of his that appeared in book form. But most of that reading was done a quarter of a century ago. I've reread a handful of the novels in recent years—*The Fabulous Clipjoint, The Screaming Mimi, Night of the Jabberwock, The Wench is Dead.* I can testify that they hold up better than much of what I was enthusiastic about twenty-five years ago, although they don't seem quite as wonderful as I remember them.

But I'm quite unfamiliar with the great mass of Brown's uncollected pulp fiction. I know precious little about his life, never met the man, and although I must have seen a photo of him at one time or another, have no sense of what he looked like.

Nor do I know any of the particulars of the novel-in-progress I'm supposed to be introducing. I don't know what Brown had in mind when he started it or what induced him to abandon it, or if he had hopes of returning to it and completing it.

So where do I get off writing an introduction?

On the other hand, how could I fail to agree? Fredric Brown was one of the writers in whose work I immersed myself at the time when I was not only deciding to become a writer but determining what sort of writer I was going to become. When the student is ready, we are told, the master will appear. Brown was one of several masters who made their appearance at a time when I was evidently ready. They taught by example, and I learned as much as I was able to learn. And what a fine time I had of it!

Thus this introduction, such as it is. Perhaps it will be rather less an introduction than an appreciation. And, at the same time, something of a thank-you note.

What a fertile mind Brown must have had! When I first read his collected short stories, I was struck by how many of them I have already encountered in anthologies. There was something special about almost all of his stories, some quality that made them linger in the mind.

I can recall a surprising number of those stories after all these years. The one that comes quickest to mind is "Don't Look Behind You," which I've always found scary in a way that is categorically different from all other scary stories. Typically, the scary story works because one forgets while reading it that one is reading fiction. The work becomes real, the reader ceases to remember that he is a reader and becomes either a character or a spectator, and whatever fear is generated dissipates when one realizes that it is, after all, only a story.

But Brown lets you know that you're reading a story, and takes pains to remind you that you're sitting there with a magazine in your hand, and scares you anyway. Yes, you're the reader, he says, and I'm the person who wrote this, and I'm behind you right now, with a knife. Hi there!

*   *   *

I never met Fredric Brown, but I certainly would have liked to. Most writers, I suspect, are a face-to-face disappointment to their fans. The reader creates his own sense of the writer's personality, while the writer, for his part, has been busy putting the most attractive elements of himself into his work. The better a writer he is, the more artfully distorted an image he may wind up presenting of himself.

Nevertheless, one senses that Brown would have been good company. His *characters* were such good company. They liked to fish, they liked to play poker, they liked to jaw the night away.

And they liked to drink. God, did they like to drink! I read most of Brown's books during that part of 1957-8 when I was living in Manhattan and working at a literary agency while writing stories for what crime pulps still existed. My hotel was the Alexandria on West 103rd Street, just two doors from the Marseilles where Cornell Woolrich (whom I never met either) was living out the end of his curious life.

One Friday night I brought home *Murder Can Be Fun* and a bottle of Jim Beam. I hadn't quite planned it that way, but whenever the lead character took a drink, so did I. Thinking back on it, it's a miracle I lived to tell the tale.

I liked the way Brown's characters thought and acted, and I liked the sense of their author that came through them—or came directly, when Brown talked straight to the reader. (I don't do that often, but it was a voice I used in some early pseudonymous work, and I know I learned it from Brown.)

I liked, too, the things that interested Brown. He had the sort of fantasies I was eager to share. I liked the newspaper backgrounds, the carnival backgrounds, the knack Brown had of taking a gritty world and peopling it with unjaded human characters. I identified with Ed Hunter, teamed with the perfect fantasy uncle to investigate his father's murder, in a wonderfully shameless interpretation of *Hamlet*. (My own attempt at a first novel, mercifully aborted around forty pages, was a similarly shameless recreation of *The Fabulous Clipjoint*.) And I wanted to follow in the footsteps of the hero of *The*

Wench is Dead, a sociology professor spending his sabbatical incognito on Skid Row and ultimately seduced by life at the bottom.

Fredric Brown's books opened windows into such alluring worlds!

And what of the book at hand?

We have here two phenomena—a novella, first published in a curious paperback format and long out of print, and an unfinished attempt to spin that yarn into a book-length novel. The novella version of *The Case of the Dancing Sandwiches* surely needs no introduction. Its author's imprint is unmistakable, and while few readers would likely argue that it was the best thing Fredric Brown ever wrote, neither was it the worst. The dialogue is lively, the characters richly human, and the story itself involving.

And what of the expanded version?

It is a curious business, taking a short work and stretching it. Interestingly enough, I am engaged at that very task even as I prepare this introduction. A story of mine ran in *Playboy* last year, and I am now extending it from eight thousand words to novel length.

I am finding this to be rather more than a matter of putting nine or ten words where one word stood, of running scenes longer, of taking time to describe settings. One might double the length of a manuscript in that fashion, but a greater expansion is called for in the present instance, and so I have added two full plot elements to the one which ran through the short story, have created and developed a number of characters who did not exist in the original, and am essentially attempting to build a whole twelve-room house around an old log cabin.

[The short story in question, I'll now add, is "By the Dawn's Early Light"; the novel is *When the Sacred Ginmill Closes.*]

Brown's novel-length version of *Dancing Sandwiches* would have inflated the story to three or four times its original length. Toward that end, he added some scenes and expanded others, but what we have here of the story line isn't greatly altered. It's interesting,

I think, that he moved his story south and west, from New York to Arizona. Perhaps he simply wanted to set the new version where he lived; perhaps he felt that a change of scene would make the process of expansion easier, that it would be easier to write whole new scenes in new settings than to stretch scenes he had already envisioned and written.

It seems to me that a plot which worked nicely in its shorter version appears on the thin side as a novel. I suspect that, had Brown initially set out to write the story as a novel, it would have grown organically, with incidents and plot complications developing en route. The process of organic growth doesn't come as automatically when one is expanding an existing work, and I think that does much to explain the thinness of the unfinished novel.

On the other hand, it's important to remember that the work is indeed unfinished, that we can't know what it might have looked like had Brown completed it. Perhaps he would simply have pushed on to the end. Perhaps he abandoned the book when he did out of the sense that it needed some structural reinforcement in order to carry the greater length.

Occasionally a piece of writing, left unfinished at death, is completed by another writer. (I once performed this service, if that is what it was, for William Ard, and I understand that more than a few posthumously published works have had this treatment, acknowledged or otherwise.) John O'Hara, I know, recoiled at the thought of another hand finishing a work of his; while this did not happen, unfinished and inferior work of his *was* published after his death, and one cannot imagine that he would have approved.

And what would Fredric Brown think of the present volume? I can't say, but I certainly don't think there's anything here for which his shade need apologize. There is good writing here, and good characters; moreover, the scholar has the rare opportunity to overlook the creative process as a piece of material is altered from one form to another.

Remember *What Mad Universe?* Imagine, if you will, a parallel world in which Fredric Brown still lives—and still writes. There's a whole shelf of books and stories of his that none of us have laid eyes on. Including this present story, its original plot elaborated and complicated, the whole work completed and polished and with an ending you wouldn't dream of in a million years.

Just imagine—

For my 1999 anthology, Master's Choice, *select writers were invited to submit two stories, a favorite by another writer and a favorite of their own. Having invited myself to the table, I chose a story of Fredric Brown's, and one of my own to keep it company:*

Fredric Brown was a purely wonderful writer, producing a substantial body of distinguished work in two genres, crime and science fiction. Reading his work, I've always been struck not only by the deceptive ease of his writing style and the startling originality of his ideas, but by the sense of the human being behind the work. It is one of my regrets that I never got to meet him.

When I began writing crime stories in the late '50s, Brown was one of the writers I devoured. I read everything I could get my hands on and found something to like in everything I read.

"Cry Silence" is one of the stories I read back then, over forty years ago. I never read it again, but I damn well remembered it, and managed to hunt it down in a friend's library the other day. There aren't many stories I recall so vividly after such a lengthy passage of time, but there are a few, and several of them had Fredric Brown's name on them.

"Sometimes They Bite" was written in 1975, during a month I spent at Rodanthe, on North Carolina's Outer Banks. There was a long pier there, and you could go out on it with a pole and fish, and that's what I did. I lived pretty much exclusively on what I hauled out of the ocean, and one day I wrote this story. Henry Morrison, my agent at the time, called a friend of mine and said he was worried about me. "I got this story from Larry," he said. "I've got a feeling he's been alone too long."

I don't know that the story owes anything to "Cry Silence," or to Fredric Brown, but I like to think it's one he might have enjoyed.

Raymond Chandler

Commissioned by GQ *for their December 1994 issue, presumably to coincide with the centenary of Chandler's birth. Except the editor got it wrong; It was Dashiell Hammett who'd been born in 1894, six years after Chandler's 1888 debut. I thought it over and wrote the article, and they ran it, and I don't know that anyone ever complained.*

"So this fellow comes into the store every Tuesday morning," Joe Bitowf said, "and buys two hardboiled mysteries. Every Tuesday, rain or shine. That's his reading for the week, and I have to tell you sometimes it's hard to find something to recommend to him, because he's been doing this for a while now."

Joe manages the ground-floor paperback department at the Mysterious Bookshop in midtown Manhattan. He's been doing it for a while, too, and if he was running out of titles to suggest, that meant that his customer was running through the books faster than the publishing industry was turning out new ones.

"He's read everybody," he went on. "All of your stuff, of course, and Estleman and Greenleaf and Valin and Parker. John Lutz. Joe Gores. Jeremiah Healy. And everybody else you can think of. *Everybody*. So he's in here the day before yesterday at his usual time and he says, 'This guy Raymond Chandler. Is he somebody I might be apt to like?'

"Can you believe it? *He never read Chandler*. And it had never occurred to me to turn him on to Chandler, because I assumed—"

"Sure," I said.

"So I sent him out of here with *The Big Sleep* and *Farewell, My Lovely.* I figured he might as well start at the beginning and read them in order. And I thought to myself, Mister, you're in for a treat."

A treat indeed, to read Raymond Chandler for the first time. I almost envied the man, even as I marveled at his having been able to defer gratification so long. How had he managed it?

"It's amazing," I said. "Chandler's the one they've all heard of, even if they haven't read anything more hardboiled than *The Bridges of Madison County.* Him and Dashiell Hammett. Chandler and Hammett, Hammett and Chandler, that's all you hear, and—"

"My God," he said. "I wonder if he's read Hammett?"

Hammett and Chandler, Chandler and Hammett. They are so often mentioned in the same breath as co-founders of a school of writing that it is easy to imagine them sharing a table in some side street dive, lighting each other's cigarettes, killing a fifth of bourbon together. Ray and Dash, plotting a new course for American crime fiction.

Never happened.

They met once, in January, 1936, at a *Black Mask* dinner in Los Angeles. Chandler had published his first story in that magazine two years earlier, around the time of publication of *The Thin Man,* Hammett's final novel. Chandler's own first novel, *The Big Sleep,* wouldn't see print until 1939. Chandler later described Hammett as "nice-looking, tall, quiet, and gray-haired, with a fearful capacity for Scotch." As far as anyone knows, they never corresponded, never spoke again.

But Chandler certainly read Hammett, and was quick to credit him in "The Simple Art of Murder" with giving a new direction to American mystery fiction. Hammett, he wrote, "took murder out of the Venetian vase and dropped it into the alley . . . [he] gave murder back to the kind of people who commit it for reasons, not just to provide a corpse . . . . Hammett is said to have lacked heart; yet the story he himself thought the most of is the record of a man's devotion to a friend. He was spare, frugal, hardboiled, but he did over and over again what only the best writers ever do at all. He wrote scenes that seemed never to have been written before."

All of this, Chandler went on, was still not quite enough. And he described the essential ingredient in a passage that seems to have defined the hardboiled hero for all time:

> "Down these mean streets a man must go who is not himself mean, who is neither tarnished nor afraid . . . . He must be a complete man and a common man and yet an unusual man. He must be, to use a rather weathered phrase, a man of honor— by instinct, by inevitability, without thought of it, and certainly without saying it. He must be the best man in his world and a good enough man for any world . . . .
>
> "He is a relatively poor man, or he would not be a detective at all. He is a common man or he could not go among common people. He has a sense of character, or he would not know his job. He will take no man's money dishonestly and no man's insolence without a due and dispassionate revenge. He is a lonely man and his pride is that you will treat him as a proud man or be very sorry you ever saw him . . . .
>
> "The story is this man's adventure in search of a hidden truth, and it would be no adventure if it did not happen to a man fit for adventure. He has a range of awareness that startles you, but it belongs to him by right, because it belongs to the world he lives in. If there were enough like him, the world would be a very safe place to live in, without becoming too dull to be worth living in."

For all their author's eloquence, I can't avoid the thought that there's something oddly self-serving about Chandler's observations. His description of the archetypical hero is quite specifically a description of Philip Marlowe, the protagonist of all seven of his novels.

Is it a description of Chandler as well?

＊   ＊   ＊

When you take a gander at his life, he doesn't come off looking
like a Mean Streets kind of guy.

He was born in Chicago in 1888 and spent much of his early
childhood in Plattsmouth, Nebraska. When he was seven his parents
divorced and his Irish-born mother took him to live with her mother
and sister in a London suburb. He had a traditional English public
school education at Dulwich, and emerged from it scribbling poems,
some two dozen of which he published in a London newspaper. At
23 he returned to the United States and settled in Los Angeles. He
enlisted in the Canadian Army in 1917 and saw combat in France,
his service ending abruptly when a German artillery barrage left him
the sole survivor of his platoon.

Back in L.A., he met Cissy—Pearl Eugenie Hurlburt Porcher Pascal—and saw her through her second divorce; four years later, and
two weeks after his own mother's death, they were married. He was
35. Cissy was 53.

He was in the oil business by then, and he rose within the company, becoming a vice president. He drank alcoholically, chased
women, and lost his job. It was 1932, he was 44 years old, and the
country was in the depths of the Depression. He decided to write his
way out of it.

He looked at the slicks—*Collier's*, the *Saturday Evening Post*.
While they paid lavishly for fiction, he found them superficial and
fundamentally dishonest. The detective pulps, and specifically *Black
Mask*, were far more appealing, and he read widely in the field, deliberately imitating established writers like Erle Stanley Gardner in
order to teach himself how to construct a crime story. His first piece
of fiction was five months in the writing; *Black Mask* bought it at
once, and Chandler was soon a regular contributor to the magazine.
By the end of the decade he had published some twenty stories, most
of them in *Black Mask*, the rest in *Dime Detective*. It was no way
to make a living—*Black Mask's* base rate was a penny a word—but
it was a good training ground. Chandler learned how to put a story

together, and he found his voice as a writer. In the process, he found Philip Marlowe.

His first novel, *The Big Sleep,* was published in 1939. Several others followed at intervals of a year or two. Then a stretch of film work interrupted the novel writing. There was a six-year gap between *The Lady in the Lake* (1943) and *The Little Sister,* and another four years before the 1953 publication of *The Long Goodbye.*

Throughout these years Chandler lived in what we have learned to call Chandler country—southern California, first in Los Angeles, then in La Jolla. Although he once called L.A. "a city with all the personality of a paper cup," his Los Angeles remains remarkably vivid, and curiously timeless. There are no drive-by shootings in Chandler's Los Angeles, no traffic jams on the Santa Monica Freeway, no houses sliding into the ocean. But the mood hasn't changed much. His landscapes have the look of bad early Technicolor, at once faded and garish, like sun-washed cereal boxes in a shop window.

You have to wonder how he got it so right. He spent a lot of time in the house—working, reading, writing letters. He saw to his wife, who required a lot of attention in her later years. And when he did get out, you wouldn't find him walking the mean streets. La Jolla, it must be noted, was never much for mean streets.

He toyed periodically with the idea of moving back to England. They certainly loved him over there. Throughout his career, his books sold as many copies in the UK as they did in the much larger American market. Chandler wanted more than anything to be taken seriously as a writer, to be perceived as the one man whose work transcended the mystery genre. It dismayed him to be reviewed by mystery critics like John Dickson Carr and Anthony Boucher. He felt he was writing Literature, and the English were more inclined to see it that way.

It is hard to know just what to make of it when one of our own is much esteemed across the Atlantic. Our first impulse is to assume the foreigners know something we don't, and then one is struck by the example of the French, and their inexplicable enthusiasm for Jerry Lewis and Mickey Rourke.

In any event, the Brits remain crazy about him, and a few of their writers have made careers for themselves as Chandler imitators, writing books set in their idea of the USA, with characters speaking out of the sides of their mouths and saying things no American ever said. Their work, popular enough at home, is unreadable over here, where every other phrase has a palpably counterfeit ring to it.

It's interesting, though, that the man who added "mean streets" to the language spent virtually no time on them; that he who wrote so eloquently about getting murder out of the English country houses was most appreciated by residents of those stately homes. Chandler did write about tough guys, certainly—sneering hoods, brutal cops, hard men. But I've always found them his least convincing creations, with much less to them than his monied Californians, venal and jaded and world-weary, living their tarnished lives in the American equivalent of the English country house.

Philip Marlowe is the hero and narrator of all seven of Chandler's novels. Chandler's body of work is not large, and one could argue that his reputation rests upon a single seven-volume novel. (He'd have produced more fiction if he hadn't hacked away at screenplays in Hollywood, but he might have starved without the screenwriting work. And he'd arguably have written more if the bottle hadn't gotten in the way; his best work was accomplished during stretches of sobriety.)

Through the first five books, we aren't given a great deal of information about Marlowe. When Robert Montgomery filmed *The Lady in the Lake,* he supplied Marlowe's voice himself while letting the camera serve as the hero. This was an interesting gimmick, even if the movie can be a little hard to watch now. It strikes me, though, that Marlowe was the perfect character for this sort of treatment. He barely owns a face or a physique in the earlier books. He is an attitude, a stance, a point of view. He is, more than anything else, the lens through which Chandler shows us the world.

In the sixth and most ambitious novel, *The Long Goodbye,* Chandler brings his hero in front of the camera. We're given a little more information about his private life and a peek into his heart and soul. This book is *about* Marlowe, and especially about his relationships with two men—his friend, Terry Lennox, and his sort-of client, the writer Roger Wade. Early on, Marlowe goes to jail rather than admit to having driven Lennox to Mexico; later, he rescues Wade from a quack sanitarium, takes him home, and makes a pass at his wife. Throughout, he alienates powerful people with his trademark wisecracks for no apparent reason, turns down fees whenever they're offered to him, and goes through abrupt mood swings that make you wonder if he shouldn't be on lithium.

Chandler was a great letter-writer, and his collected correspondence makes fascinating reading. One of his most remarkable letters was written while he was at work on *The Long Goodbye*. In response to a fan, Chandler wrote over 2000 words about the history and personal habits of Philip Marlowe.

Chekhov wrote somewhere that a writer ought to know everything about his characters—diet, medical history, shoe size, etc. Chandler, in his letter to D. J. Ibberson, describes Marlowe's apartment down to the last piece of furniture, reports on his education and birthplace, and lets us know what movies he likes to watch and what kind of booze he prefers to drink. It is hard to believe that all this was written with no greater purpose than the enlightenment of Mr. Ibberson. Chandler was almost certainly writing to himself, willing himself to see Marlowe far more vividly and completely than he had previously done.

I've just reread *The Long Goodbye* after not having looked at it in years. I'd remembered it as flawed, but found it even more confused and confusing than I recalled. A particularly striking moment comes when Eileen Wade, whom Marlowe earlier kissed for no discernible reason, for no more reason now throws herself headlong at him. Here's how he preserves his virtue:

> "Putting my arms around her I touched bare skin, soft skin, soft yielding flesh. I lifted her and carried her the few steps to the bed and lowered her. She kept her arms around my neck.

She was making some kind of a whistling noise in her throat. Then she thrashed about and moaned. This was murder. I was as erotic as a stallion. I was losing control. You don't get that sort of invitation from that sort of woman very often anywhere.

"Candy saved me. There was a thin squeak and I swung around to see the doorknob moving. I jerked loose and jumped for the door. I got it open and barged through it and the Mex was tearing along the hall and down the stairs. Halfway down he stopped and turned and leered at me. Then he was gone.

"I went back to the door and shut it—from the outside this time. Some kind of weird noises were coming from the woman on the bed, but that's all they were now. Weird noises. The spell was broken.

"I went down the stairs fast and crossed into the study and grabbed the bottle of Scotch and tilted it. When I couldn't swallow any more I leaned against the wall and panted and let the stuff burn in me until the fumes reached my brain.

"It was a long time since dinner. It was a long time since anything that was normal. The whiskey hit me hard and fast and I kept guzzling it until the room started to get hazy and the furniture was all in the wrong places and the lamplight was like wildfire or summer lightning. Then I was flat out on the leather couch, trying to balance the bottle on my chest. It seemed to be empty. It rolled away and thumped on the floor.

"That was the last incident of which I took any precise notice."

It's no trick to find passages to make fun of. One can hardly demand that a wisecrack retain its snap for forty or fifty years. Chandler sometimes seems stale, too, simply because he has been such a powerful influence on his successors. Like the schoolgirl who thought Shakespeare overrated because his plays are cliché-ridden, we can raise an eyebrow at Marlowe's world-weary cynicism because we've heard it all before. And indeed we have, but Chandler wrote it first.

A couple of generations of fictional private eyes have since worked their variations on his theme.

For all that's wrong with it—it's too long, it doesn't make sense, the ending's implausible—*The Long Goodbye* remains my favorite. Chandler found it significant that Hammett's favorite book, *The Glass Key,* is "the record of a man's devotion to a friend." So indeed, at least as significantly, is *The Long Goodbye.*

Chandler's career was essentially over after *The Long Goodbye.* Cissy was in her last illness by the time it was published, and died in late 1954. Chandler never recovered from her death. His last novel, *Playback* (1958), is a very weak book. When he died the following year, he left behind the opening chapters of an eighth novel, in which a very tired Marlowe has married Linda Loring (from *The Long Goodbye*) and become a part of the country-club set he made such a point of despising. (Robert B. Parker, a devout fan of Chandler's, later completed the book, *Poodle Springs,* in what seemed to me an ill-advised if well-meant act of homage.)

And what endures? His books, of course, still wonderfully readable after all these years. His influence, surely, stamped indelibly along with Hammett's on the whole hardboiled school of American crime fiction.

Even more lasting and influential, I submit, is his heroic attempt to lift his writing from a commercial genre to a level of pure literature. Eugene V. Debs, the longtime Socialist leader, once announced that he wanted to rise "with the ranks, not from them." Raymond Chandler wished to rise not with but from the ranks of mystery writers. He wanted to write character-driven novels, wanted to be free to include scenes and conversations and observations that did little to propel a plot. He liked comfort, but didn't much care about wealth. What he most wanted, what he dared aspire to, was greatness.

I'd argue that he achieved it. More important, he taught those who came after him that they too could set their sights that high. He rose from the ranks, and those ranks continue to ascend in his wake.

Mary Higgins Clark

Written for Mystery Scene's *tribute issue. I can't imagine anyone ever having trouble finding nice things to say about Mary . . .*

There's something about Mary.

I'm putting that in the first line on the chance that someone's probably already pre-empted it for a title. It's an inevitable choice, given the exposure the film got. But I think I might have led off that way film or no film, because there really is something indefinable and quite remarkable about Mary Higgins Clark.

Crime fiction writers tend to be a surprisingly collegial lot, marked by great generosity of spirit. (Writers in the mainstream, and in exalted lit'ry circles, have all the generosity of spirit of the wolverine. I knew one writer of bestsellers, Robert Ludlum, who got a phone call from another, Robin Cook, crowing over the terms of his latest book deal. Rather than congratulate his friend, Ludlum yanked his phone out of the wall and hurled it across the room. And Stuart Brent, a Chicago bookseller told me how he'd been interviewed for a profile of John Updike, and was quoted as saying Updike was one of the finest writers of his generation. Saul Bellow called him when the piece appeared. "I thought you were my friend," he said. "You son of a bitch, I'm never speaking to you again.")

In crime fiction, though, we tend to like one another, and to say nice things about one another. Most of us realize, I think, that we're not really in competition with each other, that we all gain whenever one of our number succeeds. While we might grin at La Rochefoucauld's observation that it is not enough to succeed, it is also necessary that one's friends fail, I don't know many of us who really feel that way.

When one of us does succeed in a colossal way, we do look for reasons. This writer, we'll tell ourselves, has managed to plug into the zeitgeist in a big way. (If nothing else, that gives us the opportunity to use the word "zeitgeist".) Another was in the right place at the right time. This one got a really strong push from a publisher who had just lost a major writer and needed to create a new one. That one has an uncanny commercial sense. And Whatsisname, who, God love him, sells like crazy for no discernible reason, well, do you suppose he may, in a past life, have removed a thorn from the paw of the Head Librarian at the great library of Alexandria—and now he's getting his reward?

Mary's success is dazzling, and of course one casts about for an explanation. Any number suggest themselves—her ability to tell a story, to create sympathetic characters, and, certainly, to come up consistently with the kind of dramatic situations that capture the imagination of the reading public. All of these are true, certainly, and all have a good deal to do with the depth and breadth of her appeal, but there's one more that may have more than a little to do with it.

People love her.

It's impossible not to. One cannot but enjoy her presence and respond to her warmth and inherent goodness. That's true in a private gathering, and every bit as true when she's in front of an audience, as she so often is.

I don't know how many times I've heard Mary speak—about her life, about her early years as a writer. It's essentially the same speech every time. (Everybody learns, sooner or later, that it's not only okay to say the same thing over and over, but that it's best that way. Writers tend to think we have to be original each time, but eventually we get over it.)

I've heard Mary's basic talk at least a dozen times, and probably twice that. And here's the thing—I always hang on every word. I'm interested in spite of myself. I pay close attention, and so does everybody else in the room.

There's something about Mary, all right, and I don't think I'm any closer to defining it than I was when I started out. And, really, does it matter? The gal's a sweetheart, and her success is towering, and she deserves—and cherishes—every single one of her millions of readers.

Joseph Conrad

A few years ago an editor at Dutton asked me if I could write an introduction to The Secret Agent, *Joseph Conrad's novel on which the Alfred Hitchcock film* Sabotage *was based. Thinking back, it strikes me that I was an unlikely choice, being not that much of a film buff and no fan at all of Conrad's. Now she couldn't have known that, but I certainly did, and I suppose my acceptance of the assignment represents, not for the first time, the joint triumph of ego and avarice over clear thinking.*

I wrote my introduction and turned it in, and avarice was satisfied though ego was not; I got paid, but the publisher dropped the project, for reasons I no longer recall. Thus the following was never printed anywhere—and while that's no great loss to the world of letters, it's nevertheless my pleasure to provide it here:

"A work that aspires, however humbly, to the condition of art should carry its justification in every line . . . . But the artist appeals to that part of our being which is not dependent on wisdom; to that in us which is a gift and not an acquisition—and, therefore, more permanently enduring. He speaks to our capacity for delight and wonder, to the sense of mystery surrounding our lives: to our sense of pity, and beauty, and pain."
—Joseph Conrad
Preface to *The Nigger of the Narcissus*

*   *   *

In the spring of 1998 my wife and I had the good fortune to sail on the *Star Flyer* from the Thai resort island of Phuket across the Bay of Bengal and the Indian Ocean, then transiting the Red Sea and the Suez Canal and disembarking finally in Greece at Piraeus, the port for Athens. The ship was a three-masted barkentine, and while she ran her engines most of the time in the interest of maintaining her schedule, she was a thing of beauty with her sails catching the wind. She had spent the winter in the seas around Singapore, and would summer in the Mediterranean, and we were on what they call a five-week repositioning cruise, with the primary object of getting her from Point A to Point B. That made it a bargain, and the ship itself and its itinerary made it a joy. We loved every minute of it.

The *Star Flyer* was registered in and flew the flag of Luxembourg—which is, you will note, a landlocked nation. The crew was the United Nations in microcosm, the dining room staff and cabin attendants largely Filipino, the ship's officers mostly German. The captain, whose name I seem to have forgotten, was German, but fluent as well in several languages, English among them. Like most sea captains I've known, he was a great reader, and his clear favorite among authors—now do you see where this is going?—was Joseph Conrad.

It was a passion he was more than willing to share. The ship's daily newspaper (an 11 x 17 sheet of paper, folded once, with a few columns of wire-service news and some data specific to the ship, like the times of sunrise and sunset, the scheduled activities, and, perhaps most important, the Cocktail of the Day) often included a quote from Conrad just below the masthead, and the captain's evening announcement, piped over the public address system, was apt to contain a pearl of wisdom from the great man.

It's not much of a stretch for a sea captain to show a fondness for this particular author, who after all made his name as a writer of sea stories, and who knew whereof he wrote, having put in many long years at sea before undertaking a second career as a novelist. Consider, too, how our captain, who grew up speaking German, and

Conrad, who grew up speaking Polish, met on the common ground of the English language; Conrad of course had chosen to write in it, and the captain chose to read the man's books (and reread them, and read them again) not in German translation but in the original English.

These considerations may have played a role early on. But our skipper's enduring passion for the books ultimately had little to do with the sea, and less to do with their author's ethnic and linguistic background. It was the stories Conrad told and the way he told them, and not least of all the truths to be found therein, that made that German captain the most ardent Joseph Conrad fan I've yet encountered. Conrad spoke, it would seem, to his capacity for delight and wonder, to the sense of mystery surrounding his life, to his sense of pity and beauty and pain.

> "What all men are after is some form, or perhaps only some formula, of peace."
> —Joseph Conrad
> *Under Western Eyes*

He was born December 3, 1857, in the Polish town of Berdyczów, and was christened Jósef Teodor Konrad Korzeniowski. His father, Apollo Korzeniowski, was a writer and translator, and when the boy was three his father was arrested for anti-Czarist political activity and exiled with his wife and son to a remote region of Russia. The mother died there; the father developed tuberculosis, was allowed to return to Poland in 1867, and died two years later.

Five years later young Jósef, set on a life at sea, traveled to Marseille to learn the ropes. He secured berths on a few ships, made a few voyages, ran guns in Spain, and raised general hell on the Marseille waterfront, which was by all accounts the right place for that sort of thing. He got into debt, and tried to get out of it by the time-honored expedient of shooting himself. The bullet missed his heart, though not by much, and he survived. The uncle who raised him helped him settle his debts, and he shipped out of Marseille in a

British freighter, intending to join the British merchant navy. But he jumped ship in London and resumed behaving badly, until his uncle straightened him out again.

This time it took. He worked for sixteen years on British ships, learning the language and the craft of seamanship simultaneously. In 1886 he both qualified for his Master's Certificate and became a British subject.

While the ideas of writing may have occurred to him earlier, it was sometime in the late '80s that Conrad began work on a novel inspired by a trader he'd met in Borneo. A four-month stay in the Congo (where he contracted the malaria from which he suffered for the rest of his life) interrupted his work, but he finished the book in due course and saw it published as *Almayer's Folly*. The following year he got married, and published a second book, *An Outcast of the Islands*, and left the sea for the dubious security of freelance writing. He spent the rest of his life in England, but moved around a good deal, perhaps with the restlessness of a longtime sailor, perhaps out of a general dissatisfaction with the world and his place in it.

While he found writing difficult and its rewards uncertain and elusive, he did win critical favor early on, and enjoyed his friendships with prominent British and American writers of his day, among them Ford Madox Ford, H. G. Wells, Henry James, and John Galsworthy. He was typed as a writer of sea stories, of course, and naturally he found this annoying, but most of his output in one way or another grew out of his maritime adventures.

The Secret Agent has been described as the sort of book Conrad would have written had he never gone to sea. It is, to be sure, a novel which owes nothing obvious to the years on open water. It is in fact an intensely urban book, a novel considerably closer in tone and spirit to Charles Dickens than *Two Years Before the Mast*.

But one could argue, I think, that, had Conrad not gone to sea, he'd very likely never have written anything at all. Had he lingered in Marseille, the next bullet, whether from his own or another's gun, would have nipped his career in the bud; had he taken some clerical job, in London or at home in Poland, how would he have found anything to write about, or developed the insight to write about anything? The sea formed him, as the war formed James Jones, and as the Mississippi formed Mark Twain.

Conrad didn't have to go to sea to write *The Secret Agent*. But he may have had to go to sea to become the man capable of writing it.

"The origin of *The Secret Agent*: subject, treatment, artistic purpose, and every other motive that may induce an author to take up his pen, can, I believe, be traced to a period of mental and emotional reaction . . . . I began this book impulsively and wrote it continuously. When in due course it was bound and delivered to the public gaze I found myself reproved for having written it at all . . . .

"The inception of *The Secret Agent* followed immediately on a two years' period of intense absorption in the task of writing that remote novel, *Nostromo,* with its far-off Latin-American atmosphere; and the profoundly personal *Mirror of the Sea*. The first an intense creative effort on what I suppose will always remain my largest canvas, the second an unreserved attempt to unveil for a moment the profounder intimacies of the sea and the formative influences of nearly half my lifetime. It was a period, too, in which my sense of the truth of things was attended by a very intense imaginative and emotional readiness which, all genuine and faithful to facts as it was, yet made me feel (the task once done) as if I were left behind, aimless amongst mere hunks of sensations and lost in a world of other, of inferior values.

"I don't know whether I really felt that I wanted a change, change in my imagination, in my vision, and in my mental attitude. I rather think that a change in the fundamental mood had already stolen over me unawares. I don't remember anything definite happening. With *The Mirror of the Sea* finished in the full consciousness that I had dealt honestly with myself and my readers in every line of that book, I gave myself up to a not unhappy pause. Then, while I was yet standing still, as it were, and certainly not going out of my way to look for anything ugly, the subject of *The Secret Agent*—I mean the tale—came to me in the shape of a few words uttered by a friend in a casual conversation about anarchists or rather anarchist activities: how brought about I don't remember now."

　—Joseph Conrad

　Author's Note, *The Secret Agent*

Well, maybe.

Conrad always insisted that he was at best dimly aware of the Greenwich Bomb outrage of 1894, but evidence places him in London at the time, and it would have had to have impact on him. It was unquestionably the direct inspiration for *The Secret Agent*, involving as it did a bomber attempting to destroy the Greenwich Observatory and quite literally hoist on his own petard when his weapon discharged prematurely.

Still, the mind of the fictioneer is a curious thing, and I've chosen to quote as much as I have above because of the insight it provides into the creative process in general and Conrad's process in particular. Whatever the incident's initial impact on his consciousness, it had had a decade and more to fade from his memory, until it had morphed from fresh news to a chunk of ore ready to be smelted into the stuff of fiction.

It is the role of the author's imagination to take every sort of experience—his own and others'—and make stories of it. *Where do you get your ideas?* ask no end of people who've never had an idea, and wouldn't know what to do with one if they did. Ideas are all over the place, no harder to come by (and no more like the finished product) than sand for a maker of silicon chips. It is what one does with an idea that is the telling thing, and that is where imagination comes in.

"Only in men's imagination," Conrad wrote in *A Personal Record,* "does every truth find an effective and undeniable existence. Imagination, not invention, is the supreme master of art as of life."

＊　　　＊　　　＊

Alfred Hitchcock's film, *Sabotage,* is based directly on Conrad's *The Secret Agent.* That seems simple enough, but it's rendered confusing by the fact that in the same year (1936) that he directed *Sabotage,* Hitchcock also directed another film called *The Secret Agent,* based not on Conrad's novel but on Somerset Maugham's novel *Ashenden, or The British Agent.* (An interesting book, incidentally, based directly on Maugham's own wartime adventures.) To complicate things further, *Sabotage* was given another title, *A Woman Alone,* when it was initially released in the United States.

I saw it recently, and found it at once a beautiful film and a silly one. The black and white composition is almost enough to make one regret the invention of Technicolor, and Hitchcock's London, like Conrad's, is loud with echoes of the London of Charles Dickens.

That's the beautiful part. There's plenty of silliness to offset it, with the love story of Sylvia Sydney and John Loder (the Scotland Yard agent, this an invention of Hitchcock's with no counterpart in the book) about as silly as it gets.

Suspense, of course, is Hitchcock's trademark, and the sequence in *Sabotage* helped make his reputation in this area. He shows us the bomb, cuts away, cuts back, cuts away, cuts back. It's a brilliant montage, revolutionary in its day, and no less effective in ours, and every time we see the damned package we're waiting for it to explode.

When it did, he damn well lost his audience. Years later, Hitchcock had this to say to Francois Truffault: "I made a serious mistake in having the little boy carry the bomb. He was involved in a situation that got him too much sympathy from the audience, so that when the bomb exploded and he was killed, the public was resentful. The way to handle it would have been for [Oscar] Homolka to kill the boy deliberately, but without showing that on the screen, and then for the wife to avenge her young brother by killing Homolka."

For all that, the film is no darker than the book, and Hitchcock peppers the script with bits of comic relief that we don't get from Conrad. There are funny moments in the book—the anarchists, for whom the dour and brooding writer had surprisingly little empathy, are a peculiar lot, and not without their amusing side. But Conrad is at heart a writer with a decidedly dark view of the world and the people inhabiting it, and this is one of the darker specimens of his oeuvre.

Hitchcock, I should note, was by no means the only person to see dramatic possibilities in *The Secret Agent*. Joseph Conrad himself turned out a stage version of the book in 1919-20, hoping to squeeze some new wine out of an old bottle. His experience as a dramatist was minimal, and the play seems not to have been much good, but it was in fact presented on the London stage in 1922. It got weak reviews, and closed after a short run. Conrad, deeply disappointed, did the right thing: he blamed the critics.

Christopher Hampton wrote and directed what everyone seems to agree was an excellent film (I haven't been able to get hold of it to judge for myself) in 1996, called *Joseph Conrad's The Secret Agent*, a title which should at least let people know what they're looking at. Bob Hoskins got good notices for his portrayal of Verloc, and he seems a perfect choice, echoing Oscar Homolka in his capacity for brooding intensity and, indeed, resembling him physically. Patricia Arquette is Winnie and Gerard Depardieu plays Ossipon.

Read the books, see the movies. Enjoy. And, as I'm sure the captain of the *Star Flyer* would approve, I'll give the last word to his favorite author:

> "Most of us, if you will pardon me for betraying the universal secret, have, at some time or other, discovered in ourselves a readiness to stray far, ever so far, on the wrong road."
> —Joseph Conrad
> *Notes on Life and Letters*

Introducing Ed Gorman

I was asked to provide an introduction for one of the two volumes of Pete Crowther's collection of Ed Gorman's work, and was happy to oblige. Beyond my fondness for Ed and his work, I owed him one—or two or three. It was as a result of his prodding that Cinderella Sims *was reprinted by Subterranean Press, and he provided that volume with a warm and thoughtful introduction himself. Here's what I came up with:*

Ed Gorman is a terrific writer, and you're going to have a wonderful time reading these stories.

Now what?

That's seventeen words. Pete Crowther, who asked me to write this introduction, has given me to understand that introductions to the volumes he publishes run in the neighborhood of a thousand words. That's not a bad neighborhood, you wouldn't be afraid to wander there after dark, but the seventeen words I've written leave me with nine hundred and eighty-seven words to write, and what am I going to write to take up the slack? I mean, I've already said everything I really have to say on the subject. *Here are some stories. Read them, and leave me alone.* What else is there to say?

Well, I'll think of something. I am, after all, a professional writer.

It is in the nature of a writer to think of something, and it is the hall-mark of a professional to then do something with it.

And meanwhile, I'm heartened by the fact that the mere process of thinking about thinking of something has stretched us to . . . ha! 187 words.

Let's see now. I've already told you to read the stories. But here's a question: Should you read them one right after the other, or should you spread them out over a period of weeks or months?

It's an interesting point. The short stories of an individual author aren't meant to be read en bloc, and may suffer from such treatment. Gulp them all down at one sitting and their inevitable similarities could make them seem stale or repetitive.

And little things can rankle. Long ago I read a collection of Flannery O'Connor's short stories, and halfway through I noticed a curious way in which she was repeating herself. A character in one story had lead-colored eyes. A character in another story had eyes the color of gun metal. And so on, and it struck me that this lady was working her way through the whole catalog of base metals. Call me, I said to myself, when you get to antimony.

On the other hand, it is when one reads a whole book of stories that a writer's themes emerge. The very similarities in stories that are essentially different give the reader an insight into who the writer is and what he's about. (And this is particularly valuable for a reader who aspires to become a writer himself. Immerse yourself in the stories of a particular writer—ideally one whom you admire—and you begin to get a clue how he does it.)

So it's up to you, Gentle Reader. Gulp these stories down, if that's your pleasure, one right after the other.

Or take your time, and spread them out over a week or a month. If you can.

469 words. Almost halfway there. I told you this would work!

*   *   *

Oh, I know what I could do. The last resort of reviewers from time immemorial. Just go through the stories, one by one, and find something to say about each of them. That's how we approached book reports in school, summarizing the plot to prove we'd read it, and reviewers still do that, and probably for that very reason.

Not I. I read all of these stories over the past week—and several were ones I'd read years before, and still reread with pleasure. But you're going to have to take my word for it. They don't need my comments, and they're not going to get them.

And even so, we're up to 596 words.

I did notice a couple of things, reading these stories. (You'll notice them yourselves, you don't need me to point them out to you, but too bad. I've got words to write here.)

There's an abiding nostalgia in many of these stories, a sweet recollection of youth in what seemed (but only seemed) a simpler, easier time. There's a glimpse of the writer in many of the young characters, of the enthusiasm for genre fiction in the boy who would grow up to write genre fiction.

There's a recurring theme of addictive behavior—alcoholism, compulsive gambling—and its unshakeable effects on the children of addicts.

And there is, most interestingly, an insistence on acknowledging the humanity of all of the characters, even the villains.

"If we could read the secret history of our enemies," wrote Longfellow in *Driftwood*, "we should find in each man's life sorrow and suffering enough to disarm all hostility."

(And yes, that's Henry Wadsworth Longfellow, the Nineteenth Century American poet whose reputation has waned over the years—unjustly, I would say. A generation force-fed "Evangeline" in grade school can perhaps be expected to dismiss its author out of hand. A look at Longfellow reveals not only a gifted and disciplined poetic craftsman but a very appealing intellect and sensibility. Do I digress? Indeed I digress, and this particular digression has brought me just past the 830-word mark.)

The secret history of our enemies. To know all may not be to forgive all, unless one is a candidate for canonization, but it does take a lot of the pleasure out of hating, doesn't it?

If Ed Gorman had never written a single story or novel, the world of American genre fiction would be the poorer for it. But his place in it would be assured all the same.

As a reviewer, as an essayist, as an editor and publisher, as a pure-D champion of the writers and writings he loves, the man has had and continues to have an enormous influence. The boy for whom Gold Medal novels were important has become a man for whom good writing remains vitally important, and he has shared his enthusiasm for it in a genuinely important fashion.

Now all that may or may not be important to you, Gentle Reader. You have a book of stories in your hand, and in a moment or two you'll get down to the happy business of reading them. But, by taking a moment to point out this other side of Ed Gorman, I've done something that's comparably important, if only to me.

I've gotten us fifty words past the thousand-work mark. So this is where I get off.

See ya!

Dashiell Hammett

This appreciation of Hammett was commissioned by the Japanese edition of Playboy *in the mid-1990s, and may well have been timed to coincide with the centenary of his birth in 1894. (GQ ordered up a piece on Raymond Chandler with the same idea in mind, but, as I mentioned above, Chandler had in fact been born in 1888.) As far as I know, the Hammett piece has never appeared in English. Indeed, for all I know it never ran in Japanese, either, as I've never seen a copy . . .*

"Write about what you know."

Anyone with an urge to write for publication is likely to hear those words of advice over and over again. According to the conventional wisdom, fiction can only be moving and convincing insofar as it is rooted in the writer's own experience and informed by his personal knowledge. While your work need not be directly autobiographical, it nevertheless must grow out of who you are and what you have witnessed.

No end of writers have taken this advice and profited from it. Soldiers have come home from war to fill books with their battlefield experience. The children of immigrants have speeded their own assimilation by distilling powerful fiction from their parents' ordeal. Men and women who have survived abusive childhoods in desperately dysfunctional families have gone on to spill their trauma upon the page, turning it into novels as an oyster turns a grain of sand into a pearl. (The image is an appropriate one; the act of writing at once cauterizes the wound and soothes the hurt, even as it produces something of beauty and of value.)

But of what use is this advice for those of us who would write escape fiction? In the fields of adventure, of mystery, of science fiction, many millions of readers have been diverted by writers who have spent whole lifetimes spinning tales out of the whole cloth. Edgar Rice Burroughs wrote about Tarzan's adventures in Africa and John Carter's on Mars, and had no more firsthand experience with the former than the latter. (He thought there were tigers in Africa.) While several ex-cops like Joseph Wambaugh and William Caunitz have turned their experience into strong and successful fiction, the outstanding police procedural series of all time is Ed McBain's saga of the 87th Precinct. Although McBain's vocational history includes such exotic jobs as a stint as a lobster salesman, he was never a policeman—but he's been able to write more than forty enduring novels over as many years about the cops of the Eight-seven.

The hardboiled private detective, the cynical loner in a trenchcoat, has become an American archetype known throughout the world. But hardly any of us who write about him have hands-on experience to draw upon. So many writers have written so many books with no greater resource than their own imaginations that it's easy to forget how it all began.

One man started it all. His name was Dashiell Hammett, and he was writing about what he knew.

Samuel Dashiell Hammett was born in rural Maryland on May 27, 1894. The family moved to Philadelphia and then to Baltimore, where he attended high school for a single semester before dropping out at 14. He held various odd jobs until 1915, when, as he later told *Black Mask*, "An enigmatic want ad took me into the employ of Pinkerton's National Detective Agency, and I stuck at that until early in 1922, when I chucked it to see what I could do with fiction writing.

In between, I spent an uneventful while in the army during the war, becoming a sergeant, and acquired a wife and daughter."

The Pinkerton organization was the unchallenged leader in its field, its symbol the unblinking eye that never slept. Founded in 1850, the agency had made its reputation solving sensational criminal cases, but by the time of Hammett's employment the agency's efforts were increasingly enlisted by western mining and timber interests to harass labor organizers, safeguard scab laborers, and break strikes.

Hammett's investigative work consisted largely of surveillance and shadowing suspects, and he must have had an aptitude for it. He became ill during the year he spent in military service, suffering from lung disease which was variously diagnosed as influenza and bronchial pneumonia, and which activated tuberculosis he had evidently contracted in childhood. After his discharge he resumed work for Pinkerton's, and continued as his health allowed. Eventually, discouraged when the premature solution of the theft of a shipment of gold cheated him out of a trip to Australia, he quit to write advertising copy for a San Francisco jeweler—and to see what he could do with fiction writing.

It was his convalescence that led him to writing. He spent days on end in the library, trying to read all the books in it, determined to give himself the education he had missed in his youth. He read widely on all subjects, and discovered that he wanted to become a writer.

He had some success almost at once, selling pieces to *The Smart Set*, a new magazine that sought to epitomize literary sophistication. His most interesting piece for that magazine was a flip, sardonic essay called "From the Memoirs of a Private Detective." It's full of ironic paragraphs and one-liners, among them the following:

"I was once falsely accused of perjury, and had to perjure myself to escape arrest . . .

"I knew a forger who had left his wife because she had learned to smoke cigarettes while he was serving a term in prison . . .

"I was once engaged to discharge a woman's housekeeper . . .
"I once knew a man who stole a Ferris-wheel."

The owners of *The Smart Set* published *Black Mask* as well.
Perhaps they steered Hammett toward *Black Mask*; perhaps, as he
would later tell his friends, he picked up a detective pulp one day
and realized he could do much better. In any event, he turned his
sights in that direction, and began almost at once to turn out the
work which would make him famous. He found a style, the tough
and gritty prose which was *Black Mask's* gift to literature. And he
found a character to give voice to that style in the person of the Continental Op.

"I didn't deliberately keep him nameless," Hammett wrote of the
Op, "but he got through 'Slippery Fingers' and 'Arson Plus' without
needing [a name], so I suppose I may well let him run along that
way. I'm not sure that he's entitled to a name, anyhow."

The Op served as Hammett's hero and narrator in two novels
and twenty-eight stories. Unlike his tall and rail-thin creator, the
Op was short and fat and middle-aged, and probably owed a good
deal to James Wright, Hammett's mentor at the Pinkerton office in
Baltimore. We never learn too much about the Op's life away from
the job, and it seems likely that he doesn't have one. Like real-life
Pinkerton agents of the time, he is on call twenty-four hours a day,
and the job seems to be his entire focus.

The Op's chief role is to investigate, to ask questions and find
out answers, but he is also called upon to stir things up and make
things happen. In "The House in Turk Street", the Op is going from
door to door looking for a missing youth from Tacoma; one of the
doors he knocks on is the hideout of a gang of criminals who've stolen $100,00 in bonds. By the time he gets out of there three of the
crooks are dead. A fourth is in custody, charged with their murder,
and the Op tells him he hadn't been investigating that case at all.

"But he didn't believe me," he adds. "He never believed me. He
went to the gallows thinking me a liar."

The Op became the quintessential hardboiled detective of fiction, a tough-minded window on a nasty world, entirely devoted to the monolithic agency that employs him. He doesn't feel much, and when emotions somehow intrude he suppresses them. Here's a revealing passage near the end of *The Dain Curse*:

> " 'You're the nicest man in the world. Except! You sat there this noon and deliberately tried to make me think you were in love with me . . . . I believed you until I came in just now, and then I saw—' She stopped.
> " 'Saw what?'
> " 'A monster. A nice one . . . but a monster just the same, without any human foolishness like love in him, and— What's the matter? Have I said something I shouldn't?'
> " 'I don't think you should have,' I said."

Dashiell Hammett wrote three non-Continental Op novels; one of them, *The Maltese Falcon,* serves as the cornerstone of his enduring reputation. John Huston's film, with Humphrey Bogart as Sam Spade and the impeccable supporting cast of Peter Lorre, Sidney Greenstreet, Mary Astor, and Elisha Cook, Jr., deserves a good measure of the credit, but here is an instance—perhaps the only instance in the history of cinema—where the book and the film are literally one and the same.

This is true not because Hammett adapted his book for the screen—he didn't—but because he wrote the screenplay when he wrote the book. Quite simply, the book is the screenplay—although you'll see John Huston credited as screenwriter. If you watch the movie, you will find nothing on the screen which does not appear in the book. Every line of dialogue, every bit of action, is just as it appears in Hammett's novel.

And, if you read the novel, you'll find nothing on its pages which is not specifically filmable. With the specific intent of making his work filmable, Hammett set out in *Falcon* to produce a work containing nothing other than what we can see and hear. While all the action is from Sam Spade's point of view, we are never made privy to his thoughts, and know them only through his visible reactions. In all the books 200+ pages, the only information we're given which could not be shown on the screen is the particular scent that issues from Joel Cairo's handkerchief.

Hammett certainly succeeded in making the book attractive to the film industry. The book was published in 1930, and when Huston's film appeared ten years later it was the third version to hit the screen. The first, originally called *The Maltese Falcon* but later retitled *Dangerous Female,* starred Ricardo Cortez, who played Spade as a smirking, slimy type. It was remade in 1936 as *Satan Met a Lady,* with Bette Davis and Warren Williams. (Arthur Treacher played Joel Cairo, and the fat man, Gutman, is played by a fat lady, Alison Skipworth.)

According to popular legend, Huston had a secretary copy the book in screenplay form so he could see how to adapt it; a studio head came upon the script, took it for finished work, and told the director to go ahead and shoot it. I can't believe it happened quite that way, but the book and script are such that the story is almost plausible.

Seeking to make his novel more filmable, Hammett achieved as well the more important end of capturing in prose the wonderful objectivity of film. Hammett's work was objective in attitude from the beginning, but the first-person Continental Op stories were quite properly seen through their narrator's eyes and informed by his perceptions. The third-person *Falcon* was different. Teachers of writing have long enjoined their students to show rather than tell their stories, and I can't imagine a better instruction manual toward this end than *The Maltese Falcon.* Everything is shown and nothing is told.

The Maltese Falcon made Hammett famous. His future seemed limitless . . . but he had only two more books to write. *The Glass Key* came a year after *Falcon,* and *The Thin Man* followed in 1934. *The Glass Key* is a strong book, and the story still holds up; curiously, it was the unacknowledged basis of a film just a few years ago, the Coen brothers' *Miller's Crossing. The Thin Man,* however, is a confused and exhausted book, the last work of a writer who had spent himself.

Throughout the '30s, Hammett made a lot of money from Hollywood and went through it as fast as he made it. Leftist politics took up much of his attention, and drink, a lifelong addiction, took an increasing toll, as his tolerance dropped while his dependence increased.

During the Second World War, tubercular and alcoholic and in his late forties, he managed the astonishing feat of enlisting in the army, and served as a sergeant in the Aleutian campaign. Afterward he returned to a climate of anti-Communist witch hunts; refusing to cooperate with a Congressional investigation, he served a term in prison for contempt of Congress. The government seized his money for back taxes. His health, never good, continued to deteriorate. He died on January 10, 1961, of lung cancer complicated by emphysema and pneumonia; the autopsy noted as well diseases of his heart, kidneys, liver, spleen, and prostate. He was buried, according to his wishes, at the national military cemetery at Arlington.

In "The Simple Art of Murder", Raymond Chandler provides the most eloquent assessment of Hammett ever written, and I wish I had room to quote it all. Hammett, he said, took murder out of the Venetian vase and dropped it into the alley; he gave murder back to the kind of people who commit it for a reason. And, Chandler said,

> "He had style, but his audience didn't know it, because it was in a language not supposed to be capable of such refinements ... Hammett's style at its worst was as formalized as a page out of Marius the Epicurean; at its best it could say almost anything. I believe this style . . . can say things he did not know how to say, or feel the need of saying. In his hands it had no overtones,

left no echo, evoked no image beyond a distant hill . . . He was spare, frugal, hardboiled, but he did over and over again what only the best writers can ever do at all. He wrote scenes that seemed never to have been written before."

And why did he burn out so quickly? Why does such an enduring reputation have such a small body of work on which to rest?

I wonder if an answer might not lurk in the one scene in *The Maltese Falcon* not to be found in the Huston screenplay. In it, Spade recounts at length the seemingly pointless story of a man named Flitcraft, who left his home and family and disappeared after nearly being killed by a beam falling from a construction site. By the time Spade succeeded in finding him, the man had recreated essentially the same middleclass life in another city with another family. Spade explains:

" 'But that's the part I always liked. He adjusted himself to beams falling, and then no more of them fell, and he adjusted himself to them not falling.' "

A beam fell and Dashiell Hammett taught himself to be a writer. Then no more beams fell, and he adjusted himself to that.

But not entirely. In 1957, an interviewer asked him why he kept three typewriters in his home in Katonah, New York. "I keep them," he said, "to remind myself that I was once a writer."

In the fall of 2014, an editor at Orion, my longtime publishers in the UK, wondered if I could find a couple of hundred words to say about the durability of crime fiction, by way of an introduction to their forthcoming edition of The Maltese Falcon. *Evidently I could:*

Detective stories aren't supposed to last. They're genre fiction, like horror and science fiction and Westerns, and everyone knows the chief characteristic of all those genres is impermanence. Oh, they're entertaining, and they'll fill an idle hour or provide relaxation at a hard day's end, but you read them and toss them aside, and you forget them, and so does the rest of the world.

Guess what? It doesn't work that way.

The world does indeed forget most books, generally in short order. The most forgettable, it turns out, are the mainstream best-sellers, those works of popular fiction that ride the zeitgeist until it bucks them off. In terms of sales, they burn brightly but soon burn themselves out.

And the next to be forgotten, curiously enough, are serious works of fiction, capital-L Literature, perhaps written in the hope of im-mortality. And some do indeed survive, largely as assigned reading for college students, but now and then actually read for enjoyment. Most, however, vanish as utterly as the pop bestsellers.

On the other hand, Rex Stout died in 1975 and Agatha Chris-tie the following year, and all of their work is readily available—and eagerly read. Edgar Allan Poe, Sir Arthur Conan Doyle, Raymond Chandler, Dashiell Hammett—I could go on, and so could you. No end of genre writers, with no higher ambition than that of putting food on their tables while entertaining their readers, have essential-ly achieved literary immortality. Not just on library shelves, not just in academic halls, but on the night tables of actual human beings. People read them—eagerly, and for pleasure.

A corner was turned a few years ago in the literary world's con-sciousness when the Library of America, a high-minded and not-for-profit enterprise, took a deep breath and brought out a volume of Raymond Chandler's novels. Chandler, of course, was the per-fect choice for such an experiment, having long enjoyed a special position in intellectual circles; donnish types liked his writing and world view so much that they were willing to overlook the fact that his books actually had stories in them, stories that gave one a reason to (shudder!) turn the pages.

A daring move, no? Well, no one sneered, or canceled a subscrip-tion. In fact, the book turned out to be LOA's sales leader, and by a wide margin. And Chandler is no longer the only genre writer in their catalogue. He's got plenty of company.

A word, before I leave you, about *The Maltese Falcon*. Three films were made from it, though the one you know—the third, with Humphrey Bogart and Mary Astor and Peter Lorre and Sidney Greenstreet and more names which you or I could reel out at a moment's notice—quite rightly eclipsed the others. As you may know, John Huston's shooting script is a line-for-line copy of Dashiell Hammett's novel.

What you may not know is that this was very much Hammett's intention. When he sat down to write it, he'd concluded that film was the medium of the future, and that a novel ought to be written so as to be readily adaptable for the screen. Accordingly, he produced a screenplay in prose form, with not a word in it that a camera could not capture.

And, while so doing, he wrote an essentially perfect novel that is every bit as praiseworthy—and no less gripping—today. If you're reading it for the first time, you have a treat in store for you. And if you've read it before, yours will be no less of a treat. This is, after all, the best sort of genre fiction, to be read and tossed aside—and picked up and read again. And again.

Hammett and Chandler are so often mentioned in the same breath that one wonders how either of them would feel about it. Each has his partisans; Robert B. Parker idolized Chandler, while Donald E. Westlake had a sky-high opinion of Hammett and a low one of Chandler. I could posit that these two writers, for all their similarities, are poles apart in that Hammett exemplifies Realism while Chandler embodies Romance. (That's Romance à la Malory, not Georgette Heyer. But you knew that, right?)

The best observation about the two that I've yet come across is James Ellroy's, writing in 2007 in The Guardian:

"Chandler wrote the man he wanted to be—gallant and with a lively satirist's wit. Hammett wrote the man he feared he might be—tenuous and skeptical in all human dealings, corruptible and addicted to violent intrigue."

Gar Haywood

I've known Gar Haywood for years, though we've never been able to spend a great deal of time in one another's company. I like him, and I like his work, and thus I was glad for the chance to write this introduction to Jim Seels's handsome edition of Gar's short fiction. As you'll see, it turned into a discourse on the changing role of the short story in the literary marketplace:

It is my pleasure to introduce you to *Lyrics for the Blues*, a collection of five excellent short stories by Gar Anthony Haywood.

That they are excellent came as no surprise to me, and should come as no surprise to you, either. Gar Haywood is a very fine writer indeed. I've read several of his novels over the years, and a couple of short stories, too, and I've never read anything of his that I haven't enjoyed. The wonder, then, is not that these stories were written well, but that they were written at all.

Because, you see, there are not many professional writers who put much time or effort into short fiction these days. In the crime fiction vineyard, where Gar and I do the greater part of our laboring, the opportunities for the short story writer are severely limited. There are two leading magazines, *Ellery Queen* and *Alfred Hitchcock*, and they are venerable institutions indeed, and play an essential role in the field of crime fiction. But the economics of the business are such, alas, that their role does not include putting a lot of money in the pockets of those who write for them.

Original anthologies constitute another opportunity for short-story writers. One is invited to contribute, and, while again the compensation rarely amounts to very much, the invitation is a fair guarantee of acceptance. But who do you suppose gets invited to contribute to these anthologies? Writers with established reputations and proven records, writers who can be counted on to deliver a good story and whose name on the cover will draw readers.

That's just the way it is, and no one's to blame for it. The fact of the matter is that there's precious little demand from the reading public for short fiction. The magazines that once published it in great quantity have either abandoned that policy or gone out of business—or, more often than not, both. You can attribute this to the emergence of paperback fiction in the aftermath of World War II, or to the rise of television a few years later; more recently, you might point to video games and the Internet as drawing readers away from all prose fiction, long or short.

But it's instructive to realize that it was not ever thus.

I'm more than ordinarily aware of the changing role of the short story just now because I'm busy putting together an anthology for Akashic Books. They've developed a virtual franchise that began with an anthology of original stories, all set in the borough of Brooklyn, with the volume called *Brooklyn Noir*. Other volumes have followed, including *Baltimore Noir* and *Los Angeles Noir* and *D.C. Noir* and, remarkably, *Twin Cities Noir*. (I suppose it's just a question of time before someone pulls together a collection of dark stories set in New York's Westchester County, for which the title *Pleasantville Noir* would seem inevitable.)

In the course of things I was enlisted to edit *Manhattan Noir*, and I was somehow able to persuade a slew of superb writers to turn out original Manhattan-based stories, all for precious little in the way of money and glory. The book garnered fine reviews and did reasonably well, and it occurred at about the same time to me and to Akashic's Johnny Temple that a companion volume (*Manhattan*

Noir 2? Son of Manhattan Noir? Manhattan Tres Noir?), itself composed not of originals but of reprints, might not be the worst idea we'd ever had.

And what a wealth of published fiction we found to draw upon! I sat down and began jotting down names: O. Henry, Edith Wharton, Stephen Crane, Damon Runyon, Cornell Woolrich, Ring Lardner, Jerome Weidman, and many more, not to mention more contemporary writers like Donald E. Westlake and Clark Howard and . . .

Never mind. You'll be able to see the whole list when the book comes out. But here's the point: several of those early writers made their reputations writing short stories, and some of them wrote nothing but short stories, and managed to make a more than decent living at it.

Consider William Sidney Porter, whom the world knows as O. Henry. In 1898 he began serving a little over three years for embezzlement, and in his Ohio prison he began writing short stories, set mostly in the Southwest and Central America. He sold them to magazines, and after his release he moved to New York, where in 1903 he agreed to provide a weekly short story for the *New York World*, for $100 per story.

Bear in mind, if you will, that this was at a time when a dollar a day was a living wage for a workingman. I don't know what multiplier to use to determine what O. Henry's stories were worth in today's dollars, but I think we can safely say that no magazine today pays anywhere near as much for short fiction as the old *World* paid O. Henry, and this for short-shorts that ran to somewhere around 1500 words.

The man never wrote a novel. Why should he?

More recently, consider Damon Runyon, who'd already distinguished himself as a newspaperman when he began making up stories about the horseplayers and rumrunners and assorted underworld types who were his companions of choice, and upon whom he so imposed his personal stamp that we now label such Broadway guys and dolls *Runyonesque*. Runyon wrote most of his stories during the Depression years of the 1930s, and sold them quite readily to *Cosmopolitan* and *Collier's* and the *Saturday Evening Post*, and received on average $5000 a story.

Five thousand 1930's dollars for a short story! And then, of course, the stories were published in book form, and the books stayed in print for years. Did the man ever write a novel? Of course not. Why would he bother?

Although his stories have outlasted almost all of the more avowedly literary fiction of his day, Damon Runyon was quite insistent that his sole objective in writing was to make as much money as possible from the pursuit. "My measure of success," he wrote, "is money. I have no interest in artistic triumphs that are financial losers. I would like to have an artistic success that also made money, of course, but if I had to make a choice between the two, I would take the dough."

If he were around nowadays, Damon Runyon wouldn't be wasting his time with short stories. If he wrote prose at all, he'd be busy populating full-length novels with the likes of Harry the Horse and Regret and Brandy Bottle Bates. More likely, he'd be pitching features and miniseries about them to studio guys and network execs.

I could go on, but I figure you get the idea. The nature of the business is such that most writers who begin by writing short fiction move on to the novel, while a great many others go directly to novel-writing and never try short stories at all. Periodically writers with established names are invited to contribute a short story to an anthology, and many of them beg off with the excuse that they've never written anything shorter than a hundred thousand words, and that they wouldn't know where to begin. Others make the effort, and sometimes it works out very well indeed, and other times the results are an embarrassment all around.

With the exception of the astonishing Edward D. Hoch, who has been producing upwards of two dozen commendable short stories a year ever since the invention of movable type, no one these days makes a career of short fiction. (Ed can write novels, and on a couple of occasions has, but realized early on that both his talent and his temperament are better suited to shorter work.) For most of us, short stories are a sideline, and one we pursue because of the creative satisfactions it provides.

Gar Haywood's stories, which you are about to read, must have been uncommonly satisfying to write. I certainly found them a treat to read. And so will you.

Evan Hunter

I had a lot to say about Evan. This first piece was for Mystery Scene's tribute issue:

Evan Hunter Was My Hero

In 1953, when I was fifteen years old, I realized for the first time that I wanted to be a writer. I had recently taken to reading serious literature, and was working my way through twentieth century American realism—Thomas Wolfe, James T. Farrell, John Steinbeck, Ernest Hemingway, John O'Hara. And I was finding a voice of my own in the compositions I was writing for eleventh-grade English class, and enjoying the approval I got from my teacher, Miss May Jepson. In one essay, a presumably humorous look at the various career choices I'd entertained since kindergarten, I concluded by observing that a review of what I'd written made one thing abundantly clear—I could never be a writer.

"I'm not too sure about that!" was Miss Jepson's response.

God bless the woman. I took one look at what she'd written on my paper and made a career choice then and there, and I've never changed my mind in all the intervening years.

That same year, *The Blackboard Jungle* was published, making its young author an overnight success. I didn't read it right away, but I was aware of it—some of the kids in school, of the handful that ever read anything, were talking about it. When I did read it, sometime the following year, I thought it was good, certainly, and I was deeply grateful that my high school was nothing like the one in the book. Aside from that, I don't recall that the book had much impact upon me.

Two other things did.

One was an article in *Writer's Yearbook,* an annual publication of *Writer's Digest.* I seem to recall that my father brought the thing home for me—he was always entirely supportive of my writing ambitions. I read it cover to cover—of course!—and was especially impressed with an article written by Scott Meredith, who was a literary agent, whatever that was. I don't recall the details, but in essence Meredith discussed his client Evan Hunter's great success with *The Blackboard Jungle.* I particularly remember a box at the end of the article that detailed the book's earnings from various sources—advance, royalties, film, etc. Evan Hunter, I was staggered to learn, had made $100,000 from the book.

Now I have no idea if that number bears any relationship to reality, and I can't offhand think of anything for which I'd be inclined to take Scott Meredith's word, but all that's beside the point. A lightbulb formed in the air above my young head, and there was a dollar sign in it. You could, I suddenly realized, make a lot of money doing this. Somehow this fact had hitherto escaped my awareness.

I don't know that I had all that much interest in making a lot of money, not in my idealistic youth. I was more interested, I seem to recall, in making my parents proud of me, and in impressing girls and maybe, God willing, actually getting laid. But I certainly wanted to be able to support myself by writing, if only to avoid having to do anything else. It was nice to know that you could.

It may have been Scott's article that led me to buy *The Jungle Kids.* I had just graduated from high school, and was still reading great writers, still planning on becoming one myself, but clueless as to how this was going to happen. I spotted this paperback on a drugstore rack, recognized the author's name, and found when I picked it up that it was a collection of short stories about what we then called juvenile delinquents. (Now we just call them young people.)

The book was a paperback original, designed to capitalize on the success of *The Blackboard Jungle,* and consisting of stories Hunter had written in the several years preceding the novel. They had been published in a variety of magazines I'd never heard of, a majority having appeared in *Manhunt.*

I read the stories, and something remarkable happened. It's not that I thought they were the best stories ever written. I thought they were damned good, and that there wasn't a clinker in the lot, but that's not the point. What struck me, really struck me, was twofold—they were perfectly good stories, and they were stories I could have written.

I don't know how effectively I can explain this. I somehow identified, not so much with the characters in the stories as with the man who had written them. I could imagine myself coming up with ideas like his and turning them into stories like those stories. I actually did get an idea for a story—a man set upon by a gang of young punks, and turning more savage than his tormentors. I tried to write it, but didn't get anywhere with it.

I went off to college and wrote various things, mostly poems. I sent them off to magazines and was not surprised when they came back. Summer of '56 I went to New York on a co-op job—my college, Antioch, had a system where you got practical experience by working half the year in various jobs they found for you. I worked in a publishing house mailroom, lived in Greenwich Village, and loved (at least in memory) every minute of it.

One weekend I wrote a story about a young man who lived by his wits, stealing from an employer, committing mail fraud. When I went back to school in the fall I took it along with me, and during the winter I came across it and decided it was pretty good. I remembered that Evan Hunter had published some stories in *Manhunt,* whatever that was, so I looked up the address and sent it there. The story itself appears in *Opening Shots,* along with the details of what I went through before it finally sold. Suffice it to say that it wound up in *Manhunt.*

And the following year I wound up working for Scott Meredith. I answered a blind ad, took a test, and dropped out of school for a year to keep the job. Evan Hunter, I learned, had had the same job, and had gone from employee to client, and was now living up in Westchester County. The industry was full of Scott's ex-employees—the place was a great training ground for future writers and editors—but Hunter was the star, the golden boy who'd gone from one of our beat-up desks straight to the bestseller list.

Interviewers like to ask a writer to name his influences. I've never cared for the question because it has never struck me as terribly applicable to what I do. Jazz musicians discuss their influences, and rightly so; one of the things you do, when you begin as a musician, is try to play like those people whose work you most admire.

But is that what a writer does? I don't think so. While I may have had any number of writers whom I greatly admired, I can't recall trying to write like them, to *sound* like them. What you try to do as a writer, it seems to me, is to *avoid* sounding like anybody else. You do everything you can to find your own voice.

In a sense, to be sure, I was influenced by everything I read. And it's fair to say I was influenced more by bad work than good; working for Scott, laboring in the agency's slush pile, I read tons of crap every day. That's how you learn, seeing what's wrong, noticing what doesn't work, learning what not to do.

How could I learn anything from Evan Hunter? The guy never wrote a bad sentence.

It has been observed—I forget where or by whom—that only kids have heroes. I'm not entirely sure that's true, but I do think you have to stop being a fan in order to become wholly a professional. You can continue to admire and delight in the work of another writer, but if you're slavish in your devotion, if you're stuck in the role of full-blown fan, your own growth will be limited.

I remain an enthusiastic reader of Evan Hunter's work. I've always enjoyed him under all his names—I discovered the first Ed McBain books before I knew who wrote them—and he's one of the writers I buy right away in hardcover, as soon as the books come out. I am more than a little in awe of some of his accomplishments—keeping the 87th Precinct series fresh after fifty books over almost as many years, for instance, and actually getting better over the years. And writing so many different kinds of books, peopled with so many different kinds of characters. And having the energy to go on writing so rapidly, so prolifically, and so well.

In recent years I've gotten to know the man, and we've become friends. It did not surprise me to find out that Evan is good company. I already knew that from the books.

You can't be friends with your hero, and I'm far too old to have heroes, anyway. But if I did have any, well, he'd be on the list.

Under several names.

And this, written shortly after his death in 2005 at the age of 78. I've no idea where it may have appeared, and Google's no help. My guess is someone asked me for a contribution for a batch of similar tributes, perhaps to be published online, and this is what I sent:

I'm not sure how long I knew Evan Hunter. A little over fifteen years would be my best guess. But he's been a presence in my life for far longer than that.

The Blackboard Jungle was published in 1953, and it was probably a few months later when I read it. I was in high school myself, but my eminently middle-class school was nothing like the one Evan was writing about. Still, the book had an impact—it was, and no doubt still is, a gripping tale well told—but it was deeply underscored by a profile of Evan that I read a few months later in a writers' magazine. I had by that time realized that I wanted to be a writer myself, and my father, quick to encourage what struck him as a laudable ambition, came across the *Writers' Yearbook* annual at a newsstand and brought it home. And I read about Evan Hunter, and how he'd gotten out of the Navy and had this job and that job, and then started writing magazine fiction, and had now achieved best-sellerdom and a movie sale.

It must have been a year or so later when I picked up a paper-back copy of *The Jungle Kids*—published and titled to cash in on *The Blackboard Jungle's* success, of course. It was a collection of stories Evan had written under various names for *Manhunt Magazine* and its legion of imitators. They were all about high school kids, and I suppose I could have identified with the characters, and maybe I did. But what I really did was identify with the author.

I'd read my way through a ton of American realism, had found much to admire in Hemingway and Steinbeck and Wolfe and Far-rell, but this was something different: reading these fairly elemen-tary stories, I could imagine myself writing stories very much like them.

Cut to the summer of 1957. I'd completed two years of college and had come to New York City to get a job. I answered a blind ad for an editorial position at a literary agency, took the test they gave ap-plicants, and aced it. They hired me. The agency was Scott Meredith, and that was where Evan had worked while writing his earliest pulp stories. Now, of course, he was writing full time, and living the life of a country squire up in Westchester County, but Scott still represent-ed him, and he was the agency's fair-haired boy, and an inspiration to all the wannabe writers who worked there.

Right around the time I got the job, I sold my first short story. To *Manhunt*, as a matter of fact.

I dropped out of school to keep the job—it was better training for my profession than anything I could get in a classroom—and I spent my free time writing stories and articles. I never met Evan during the nine months or so that I stayed there. I didn't meet anybody; clients used a private entrance and went to see Scott without passing through the bullpen where we employees were laboring. But he did buy me a drink.

That Christmas of 1957, Evan sent splits of champagne to all of us in the back room. I thought it was the most remarkable act of generosity. Everybody got a bottle, and I drank mine on New Year's Eve. Mumm's, it was. Don't ask me why I remember that, but I do.

It occurred to me that I ought to thank him, but by the time I got the chance, some thirty years later, I have to admit it slipped my mind. By then I'd long since outgrown my hero-worship, although I'd never ceased to be an enthusiastic reader of everything the man wrote. I don't recall just when we met, but it would have been at a party, or possibly at one of the Mohonk Mystery Weekends that Don and Abby Westlake were running. Over time we became good friends, and it felt a little strange, because this was someone I had so long admired, and now we were friends. I found this enormously gratifying.

Evan was a remarkable writer, as everyone else writing these tributes will assure you. He never once wrote a bad sentence or a dull paragraph, and he never lost his enthusiasm for the lonely chore of putting words on paper. His 87th Precinct novels are a towering achievement, over fifty of them, spanning half a century, and not merely sustaining their early excellence but improving upon it, as he was able to write longer and more complicated novels in the series.

Did I mean to end it that abruptly? Or was there more once? Never mind. I got to write about Evan at much greater length in a pair of 2011 Mystery Scene *columns, and began by repeating the story of the champagne. I guess it made quite an impression:*

Long before I first met Evan Hunter, he bought me a drink.

I remember it well. It was champagne, Mumm's Brut, and it was one of half a dozen bottles that he sent to the office at the Scott Meredith Literary Agency. It was Christmas, 1957, and I'd been working there since a bemused fellow at Qualified Employment sent me over there in August to take a blind test.

The test consisted of reading a story ("Rattlesnake Cave") and writing a letter to its author ("Ray D. Lester"). One could tell the author the story was fine, or suggest revisions, or explain why it stank.

Ray D. Lester was in fact the science fiction writer Lester Del Rey, and he'd written the story to Scott's order, striving to encompass every plotting flaw he could think of. I pointed them out in my letter, and got the job, which consisted in doing essentially the same thing forty hours a week, with other stories that were every bit as bad as "Rattlesnake Cave," but not by design.

They hired me in spite of both my youth—I had just turned nineteen—and the fact that I'd be going back to Antioch College on the first of October. They didn't know that part, and I figured I'd cross that bridge when I came to it, but after two months I burned it instead and told the college I wouldn't be coming back after all. It was the best job in the world for me, and I could write a whole column about the place, and will, but this one is about Evan Hunter.

Our office was on the eighteenth floor at 580 Fifth Avenue. A couple of years later Scott moved to more spacious quarters on the seventh floor, but on eighteen there were just six of us hirelings in the outer office, and everybody got a bottle. Champagne bottles come in a great variety of sizes, and each size has a name all its own. There are Magnums and Jeroboams and Mehuselahs and Nebuchadnezzars, and don't they sound grand? There is also the split, which contains just enough champagne to fill two glasses, and that's what each of us got, and I couldn't have been happier.

I saved it for New Year's Eve. A date and I could each have had a glass, but I didn't have a date, so I drank the whole bottle.

I read *The Blackboard Jungle* in high school, probably within a year of its 1954 publication. I was reading a rich diet of Steinbeck and Wolfe and Farrell and O'Hara, and I can't say Evan's novel blew me away. I thought it was okay, certainly, but it didn't make kneel in homage.

My next contact with the man, albeit from a distance, was when my dad brought home a copy of *Writer's Yearbook*. Scott Meredith had contributed a self-serving article, explaining just how much money Evan had made from *Jungle,* how he'd sold film rights in advance of publication, and all the other great deals he had made on his author's behalf. I think the total sum ran to $100,000.

That impressed me, but I can't say it made me salivate. I knew by then that I was going to be a writer, that I'd somehow produce books and stories, and that I'd somehow make a living doing this.

Then, some months later, I bought a paperback at a drugstore. It was *The Jungle Kids,* a collection of stories Evan had original-ly published in magazines, mostly *Manhunt*. They all had youthful protagonists, and they'd been collected to cash in on the success of the novel.

I thought they were terrific. And I had a solid experience of iden-tification—not with the juvie characters, but with the author him-self. Because the two things that struck me about what I was reading were (a) that these were genuinely good, and (b) that I could see myself writing them.

And I immediately got an idea for a similar story, and sat down and tried to write it. It was terrible, and died a few pages in, and I threw it out and forgot about it.

But when I sold my first story, it was to *Manhunt*. When I got a job good enough to quit school for, it was where Evan started; he'd gone to work for Scott when the office was even smaller, and had been good enough at it that the Meredith brothers had talked about making him a partner. Instead he'd done well enough writing to devote himself to it full-time, and when I started there he was the agency's star client—which is why *noblesse oblige* led him to send some champers to the wage slaves.

Do you think I minded that I didn't have a date? Or that two sips of Mumm's don't make New Year's Eve any more than two swallows make a summer? What, are you kidding? Evan Hunter bought me champagne!

Let's talk about names.

He was born Salvatore Albert Lombino, and his first sale was a science fiction story bylined S. A. Lombino. His employer, whose name at birth was a far cry from Scott Meredith, convinced him that an Italian name was an impediment to success, and Evan Hunter was born out of his high school (Evander Childs) and college (Hunter). There were other pen names during those pulp years—Hunt Collins, Richard Marsten—but Evan Hunter was first among them, and he hadn't been using it long before he went to court and made it official.

When I worked at Scott Meredith, the receptionist, an Englishwoman named Joan, still called him Sal. "It's Sal on line one," she'd inform Scott. And at his memorial service half a century later, a sister of Evan's indicated that he was still Sal to her.

Everybody else called him Evan. It annoyed him that some people felt he was sailing under false colors, or ashamed of his Italian heritage. His enduring series character was Steve Carella, and Evan wrote about him with great success for fifty years. Evan's early years were spent in Italian East Harlem, and he used that background in one of his finest novels, *Streets of Gold,* narrated by a blind Italian-American jazz pianist. He was open enough about who he was, but he felt that one's name was a matter of choice. You could keep the one you were born with or pick one that better suited you, as you preferred.

When Ed McBain's Eighty-seventh Precinct novels outperformed Evan Hunter in the marketplace, Evan found himself addressed as Ed by fans and interviewers. He didn't mind. But he knew who he was. He was Evan Hunter.

Before he started writing, Evan thought he'd be an artist. He was good enough at it to win an Art Students League scholarship and to be admitted to Cooper Union. He started writing stories during his World War II naval service, and was to say that as an artist he had seen everything in a frame, and later came to see everything with a beginning, a middle, and an ending.

The job with Scott Meredith made him a writer, but it's hard to believe he ever considered doing anything else. Evan loved to write, and it was something he could do rapidly and well. He turned out an extraordinary volume of work, and never lost his enthusiasm for it.

In his mid-seventies, after a couple of heart attacks, an aneurysm, and a siege of cancer that had led to the removal of his larynx, Evan did something that sums up the man. He decided that what the reading public most wanted was books about women in jeopardy, so he sat down and, as Ed McBain, wrote *Alice in Jeopardy*. And went to work right away on *Becca in Jeopardy,* with every intention of working his way through the alphabet.

Don't you love it? Here's a man with one foot in the grave and the other on a banana peel, and he's perfectly comfortable launching a twenty-six book series.

The Dean Hudson novels give further evidence of Evan's enthusiasm for the task of stringing words together.

In the late '50s the genre of soft-core erotica was born, and a number of us found it to be a well-paying apprenticeship, and a very forgiving medium in which to find oneself as a writer. Along with Don Westlake and Robert Silverberg, I became a steady producer of pseudonymous books. (We called them *sex novels;* today's term seems to be *erotica,* and I must say I like that better; I feel like Moliere's character who is startled and rather pleased to discover that all his life he's been speaking prose. Damn! I've been writing erotica!)

The foremost publisher of this erotica was Bill Hamling, whose imprints included Nightstand Books and Midnight Reader, and Scott Meredith had an exclusive deal to feed Hamling a steady supply of manuscripts. (Scott got 10% of what his writers were paid, of course, and we've since learned he also got a packaging fee of $1000 a book. So when I wrote a book for $1000, I received $900 and my agent pocketed $1100. What a guy!)

By this time Evan was a best-selling author with an estate in Pound Ridge, up in Westchester County. He was writing about Carella and the guys in the Eight-Seven, and he was writing mainstream fiction as Evan Hunter, but he had time on his hands. He told Scott he could certainly spare a few days each month to knock out a book for Hamling.

And the extra dough would come in handy, because no one but Scott would know he was writing the books, and Scott would pay the money into a special account, which Evan could then use to pay the expenses of the girlfriend his then wife didn't know about.

Thus Dean Hudson, a pen name not too hard to decipher; Evan lived on or near the Hudson River, and was certainly entitled to see himself as the dean of Hamling's faculty of eroticists. I don't know how many books he wrote as Dean Hudson; somewhere along the way he tired of the sport, or perhaps broke up with the mistress, and Scott, never one to let go of a good thing, found some young hopeful to ghost Dean Hudson books, even as Don and I enlisted various up-and-comers (or down-and-outers) to write under the banners of Andrew Shaw and Alan Marshall.

Evan always refused to acknowledge that he'd written as Dean Hudson. He insisted, to interviewers and on his website, that he'd had nothing to do with the books. I don't know what he might have said privately because the subject never came up between us.

While Evan hit the bestseller list a couple of times, it frustrated him that he didn't sell better. Men and women who couldn't write their names in the dirt with a stick were hitting the list all the time, and he wasn't, and he couldn't understand why. Once he and Don Westlake were on a plane together, lamenting the fact that neither of them was writing the sort of book that had a real shot at bestsellerdom. They agreed that each would make a special effort to come up with a genuinely commercial idea, and before the plane landed Don told Evan triumphantly that he'd done the trick. The perfect can't-miss idea had come to him.

The idea? The narrator's an angel, sent to earth on a mission. Don wrote the book, called it *Humans*, and three or four people went out and actually bought it.

So much to say, so little space. Tune in next issue for the rest of the story . . .

And the rest appeared the following month:

In the marketplace, Ed McBain largely eclipsed Evan Hunter. I don't know how much this may have irked Evan. He took the work under his own name more seriously, but he took the Ed McBain books seriously enough, and indeed wrote twenty of them and not a single Evan Hunter novel in the ten years between *Lizzie* (1984) and *Criminal Conversation* (1994). He never tired of writing them. (Or I of reading them; I can't think of another series that lasted so many years, ran to so many volumes, and maintained such a consistently high level of quality.)

Still, Evan delighted in telling how he'd met Dina, the woman who would become his third wife, in a bookstore. When she learned his name, she enthused over his books. *Strangers When We Meet, The Chisholms, Streets of Gold, Last Summer, Buddwing* . . . she'd read them all, remembered all their details, and was a devoted fan.

But, he loved to point out, she knew him only as Evan Hunter. She'd never heard of Ed McBain!

Candyland seems to me Evan's most remarkable book, and his most personal one. He billed it as a collaboration between Evan Hunter and Ed McBain, and if that strikes you as gimmicky, well, it's nevertheless a legitimate description. Half the book tells the grim and desperate story of a compulsive sex addict who winds up accused of murder. That's the Hunter half. The McBain portion consists of the Eighty-seventh Precinct's investigation of the case.

I'd say this was a book Evan had to write, and he may have needed to bring the twin personae of Hunter and McBain to bear on it. While he strove for discretion in his personal life, enough anecdotes circulated to make it clear that the problem of *Candyland's* protagonist was shared by its author.

I'll tell just one story, because it's one nobody else is likely to know. I heard it from a media escort, who was discreet enough to mention no names; something else she'd said in another context allowed me to decode the story, to her considerable dismay.

But it's too good to miss. She was escorting Evan in Denver, taking him to bookstores and interviews, and after a couple of hours he suggested that the day might best conclude with an intimate dinner at his hotel. "And I don't want you to think that I hit on escorts," he assured her. "I'm on the road once or twice a year, and I swear this is the first time I ever . . ."

She let it go, and turned him down gently. And told me how hard it had been to keep from saying, "Yeah, right. Then how come three nights ago you fed that line word for word to my stepmother in Cleveland?"

That Evan was able to address the topic of sex addiction in *Candyland*, and that he did so as directly and effectively as he did, suggests that he'd already addressed and dealt with it in life. The Serbian woman who knew Evan Hunter but not Ed McBain probably had something to do with that. Marriage to Dragica Dimitrijevic (whom I have known as Dina) changed him. He seemed much happier.

The change manifested itself publicly in one curious way. From the time they found each other, Evan dedicated every book he wrote to Dina. In at least one dedication, he went so far as to apologize for the repetition, saying that he knew this was getting boring, but nevertheless . . .

I don't know that anyone else cared, or even noticed, but the change had an ironic impact upon me. Back in my days at Scott Meredith, when I read each of his novels as soon as it appeared, I always noted the dedication. Evan was always a very prolific writer, and each dedication was to a different individual or couple. It was remarkable, it seemed to me, not only that he could write so many books, but that he never seemed to run out of people to whom they could be dedicated.

And I allowed myself to entertain the schoolboy fantasy that some day Evan and I would become friends, and he'd dedicate a book to me.

Then I forgot about all of this, and time passed, and Evan and I became acquaintances, and over a few more years that ripened into friendship. I remembered my youthful fancy and realized that it might actually come to pass. The man was as productive as ever, and we were friends now, so it was not unreasonable to suppose that my turn as dedicatee might sooner or later arrive.

By then, of course, I'd largely grown out of caring about that sort of thing. I'd had a couple of books dedicated to me, and I was not unappreciative of that sort of thing, but I'd dedicated enough books of my own for the bloom to be off that particular rose. Still, given the unwitting role the man had played in my own personal mythology, well, to have Evan dedicate a book to me would represent some sort of triumph.

When *Hit Man* came out, I dedicated it to Evan. If this was a manipulative act on my part, I have to say it was wholly unconscious. I had a book to dedicate, and he was a friend who I thought would enjoy Keller. I wasn't expecting reciprocity. The dedication read "For Evan Hunter." It didn't say *R.S.V.P.*

Still, I could hardly avoid having it in mind that eventually it would be my turn in the barrel. I didn't really think about it, and then as each succeeding book was dedicated in its turn to Dina, I realized it wasn't going to happen.

No matter. I treasured his friendship, not only for the pleasure of his company but it told me how far I'd come. I didn't need a dedication to remind me. I was in no danger of forgetting.

Sometime in the late '60s, Evan left Scott Meredith. The break was probably inevitable, but what precipitated it was Scott's having made innumerable photocopies of a manuscript of Evan's for film submission. Nothing came of it, and Scott charged Evan $1100 for photocopying, all without ever having consulted him. That sounds like a hefty sum now, and was a good deal moreso in 1967. Evan blew up, and called it quits.

Scott died in 1993, and as soon as Evan got the news he started calling his friends. "Did you hear the news? Scott died! Scott is dead! Isn't that great? Isn't that the best thing you've ever heard?"

Now I was aware that the end of that particular author-agent relationship had not been entirely amicable, but at the time Evan's reaction seemed just the slightest bit extreme. Much later I learned he had his reasons.

Evan was going through a divorce from his first wife at the same time that he was attempting to extricate himself from Scott. At one point Scott picked up the phone and called the first Mrs. Hunter. "You and I have interests in common," he told her, "and perhaps ought to join forces." Whereupon he divulged no end of personal and financial details—about the mistress, for example, and all those unrecorded payments made to the Dean Hudson account.

Evan constantly generated ideas, and not all of the were for books. It must have been sometime in the late '90s that he came up with the notion for "Grand Jury."

As he saw it, it was to be a television program, most likely for cable. It would consist of himself, Don Westlake, and me, all of us MWA Grand Masters (hence the Grand) discussing and judging the work of other writers (thus the Jury). He figured it would be great fun for the three of us, who'd already established that we enjoyed one another's company, and that it would generate enormous publicity for our own work, and make us all rich and famous.

We had a few meetings toward this end. Once, I remember, we sat down for lunch with my good friend Patrick Trese, a distinguished writer and producer of TV news and documentaries, and discussed the form the show could take and the possibility of Pat's producing it. Another time producer Richard Rubinstein took an interest, and set up a meeting with a couple of young guys from one of the cable stations. They seemed pleased to be in the same room with the three of us, but couldn't quite pull off the trick of appearing interested in Evan's idea.

I don't know that Don or I believed for a minute that this would work. Who would put it on the air? And, if someone did, who would watch it? But that doesn't mean either of us entertained the notion of saying as much to Evan. His enthusiasm was enough to keep us on board.

Besides, who knew? Maybe he could bring it off.

Consider *Transgressions*. After no end of invitations to edit an anthology, Evan decided just what kind of an anthology he'd do. He wanted ten prominent authors each to do a 20,000-word novella. And, in order to get us all on board, he wanted assurance that we'd all be well compensated for our trouble. I'm not positive of the figure, but I believe we were to get $20,000 apiece.

If anyone else had proposed this, you'd have to figure he was just trying to get out of editing anything, ever. A publisher was going to have to come up with $200,000 in front—plus whatever Evan was getting as editor. Big names or no, that's daunting. And the book itself, at 200,000 words, would be expensive to produce and probably too costly to sell well.

And how were you going to get the big names on board, anyway? Yes, the money was decent enough, but a 20,000-word hunk of fiction is an impossible length to market. If the deal fell through, if the publisher backed out, what on earth could you do with the damn thing? Cut three-fourths of it and peddle it as a short story? Pump another fifty thousand words into it and call it a novel?

Well, go figure. Don and I turned in stories, of course, and so did Jeffery Deaver, Joyce Carol Oates, Anne Perry, John Farris, Sharyn McCrumb, Walter Mosley, Stephen King . . . and one Ed McBain. Forge published it, and did well with it, and a slew of overseas sales brought in some more dollars (well, yen and euros, anyway) for all concerned.

I don't honestly think anyone but Evan could have made this happen. And, now that I think about it, I have to wonder if those cable guys missed the boat. Maybe "Grand Jury" could have worked. If Evan thought it could, who am I to say it couldn't?

Transgressions came out in April of 2005. Three months later, the cancer that had taken Evan's larynx took his life. (He wrote about his illness in a memoir called *Let's Talk,* an extraordinary book that somehow didn't get published in the States; Orion brought it out in the UK two months before his death.)

Evan wanted to go on living. He had a wonderful marriage, he had a fine career, and he was able to write. In a late interview, he talked cheerfully about planning to live to be 104. I don't know if he believed this, or to what extent he saw the end coming.

We who knew him were aware the end was imminent; because we knew what he'd been going through, we could only regard his death as a mercy, even as we regretted the loss.

A while later, Dina had *Becca In Jeopardy* sent to me, with the thought that I might undertake its completion. I was honored to be selected, and felt that such an enterprise was not one Evan would find unwholesome; back in 1959, he had completed *The April Robin Murders,* which Craig Rice had left unfinished.

But when I read what he'd left, I decided the few chapters and several pages of amorphous notes weren't something I could turn into a book that would do either of us credit. I don't doubt that Evan could have made it work, but that was because it was a story of his devising and he had an idea where he was going with it. I said as much to Dina, and she was persuaded to trust my judgment rather than look for another writer.

I'd have liked to finish my friend's book. But I'm grateful I decided not to try. It's not as though he doesn't have enough books to his credit—and not a dull page, a lifeless paragraph, or an ungainly sentence in any of them.

One writes differently, more freely, about the dead. I told a few tales here I'd never have considered telling during Evan's lifetime. Was this disloyalty? Ah, well. Not for me to say.

Henry Kane

"Remembering Henry Kane" was one of my Murders in Memory Lane columns for Mystery Scene:

Henry Kane's pretty much forgotten these days, with all his work out of print. You can Google him, as I did, and you'll unearth a great deal of information that way, some of it true. And you can find copies of his books on eBay and Amazon and other used-book sources. He wrote over sixty novels, and while none of them hit any bestseller lists, there were enough copies printed so that some survive.

He was born in 1918, earned a law degree, but if he ever practiced the profession he gave it up when he found he could make a living with a typewriter. He wrote a great deal over the years for radio and television, and probably created the series "Martin Kane, Private Eye," which had a good run on both media. The Blake Edwards TV show, "Peter Gunn," was clearly inspired by Kane's series of books about one Peter Chambers, though Kane never got any official credit.

I read his stories in *Manhunt*, and his books, when I began trying to write crime fiction of my own. In the first or the third person, Kane wrote with no apparent effort and produced narrative that was sophisticated, amusing, and urbane. I haven't read anything of his in ages, and the books I once owned have long since moved on to other owners, but I remember having enjoyed them all.

I came to know him through our mutual agent, another Henry—Henry Morrison. I spoke with Henry Morrison recently, and learned that it was at HK's urging that HM opened up shop as an agent back in the mid-'60s.

HM had decided to part company with Scott Meredith, for whom he'd worked for almost ten years, and was planning to sign on as an editor at a paperback house. He said as much to Kane, who took him out to dinner and told him he was making a mistake and wasting years of great experience. He should open his own agency, Kane said, and that way he'd be doing what he was best suited to do, and working for himself, and would no doubt blossom as an excellent agent.

And would Kane go with him?

"No," said Henry Kane. "Because you might not make it, and then where would I be? But set up on your own, and get yourself some clients, and if you're still in business a year later, *then* I'll go with you."

And that's what happened. Henry Morrison became a successful agent, and after a year Henry Kane became his client, and never left. I met Kane a couple of times when we were both visiting HM's office to drop off a manuscript or pick up a check, and in the early '70s we got to know each other. I was living on 22 acres outside of Lambertville, New Jersey, and had a fourth-floor walkup studio on West 35th Street between Fifth and Sixth Avenues that I used for writing and adultery. (I was far more successful at the former pursuit, and wrote several books there, including *Ronald Rabbit is a Dirty Old Man* and *Chip Harrison Scores Again*.) Henry Kane lived on Long Island—Lido Beach, if memory serves—and spent Monday through Friday in an apartment on 34th Street west of Ninth Avenue.

I paid a few visits to his *pied-a-terre*, and had some good conversations. He took his work seriously, and insisted that each page be perfectly typed before he went on to the next one. He began the work day by swallowing a Dexamil capsule, and after a certain number of hours at the typewriter he'd pour himself a little Scotch to soften the edge of the speed. He'd sit there typing and chain-smoking and sipping Scotch until the day's work was done, and then he'd go out for dinner and a night on the town.

Uh, don't try this at home.

At one point, according to Kane, his wife began to worry that his lifestyle was going to kill him. She got him to go to a doctor, who put him through a thorough physical. When the results were in, the three sat down together, and Mrs. Kane waited for the doctor to put the fear of God into her husband.

"I understand you drink," the doctor said.

"Scotch," said Kane.

"How much?"

"About a quart a day. Sometimes more, if I make a night of it."

"And you smoke cigarettes."

"A couple of packs a day."

"And you take Dexedrine."

"As prescribed," said Kane. "A pill every morning. Sometimes, but not often, a second pill as a sort of pick-me-up."

The doctor looked thoughtful.

"Tell him," said Kane's wife. "Tell him what he's doing to himself. Tell him he absolutely has to stop."

"Ah," said the doctor. "Well, Mr. Kane, I have to say you're in perfect health. I wouldn't recommend your regimen to anybody else, but it seems to be serving you well."

That, at least, is how Kane recounted the incident to me, with enormous glee. I suspect what the doctor said was more along the lines of *Well, it hasn't killed you yet*—but one hears what one wants to hear.

But I'll say it again: Don't try this at home.

There are two stories Henry Kane told me that have no bearing on his work, and are in no way instructive to young writers. But they're the reason I chose him as the subject for this column—along with the fact that he was far too entertaining a writer and far too engaging a gentleman to be entirely forgotten.

Kane was in his early fifties when I got to know him, and some years previously his father had died. And ever since then, Kane had heard footsteps.

Not all the time, to be sure. But every now and then he would hear someone pacing the floor overhead, walking back and forth, back and forth. At first he'd thought there was in fact someone up there, but it even happened when he was on the top floor, or sitting home in an otherwise empty house. It became clear that he was hearing these footsteps, and there were no feet responsible.

He also discovered that other people didn't hear them. He most often heard them when he was alone, but sometimes there would be other people present, and they couldn't hear the footsteps, not even after he'd called them to their attention.

He spoke about this to a woman who asked him a few questions, established that Kane was a Jew and the son of a Jewish father, and that he'd never heard the footsteps until after his father's death. "Well, the footsteps are your father," she told him. "His soul can't rest until someone says Kaddish for him. You haven't done that, have you?"

No, Kane said. He hadn't. He didn't believe in any of that mumbo-jumbo.

"Fine," she said, "You don't have to believe in it. Just get your ass to a synagogue and say the prayer when the time comes. It's in Hebrew—well, Aramaic, actually—but it's transliterated, so you just read it."

"And if I do that?"

"Then the footsteps will stop."

"That's ridiculous."

"So try it. What have you got to lose?"

But he wouldn't.

His was a curious sort of obstinacy. It's not that he didn't believe her suggestion would work. He was the one telling the story, and it was evident to me that he figured she was right, that he could get the footsteps to stop by spending a few minutes muttering something incomprehensible in a dead language. And he did indeed want those footsteps to stop.

But not enough to part with his own principles, whatever exactly they may have been. If he did it, and if it worked, well, then where would he be? So the elder Kane went on pacing, and Henry went on hearing him.

Did I mention that he was a Taurus?

Henry knew a lot of people, and traveled in sophisticated circles. While he was hardly a matchmaker, he sometimes introduced one friend to another, thinking they might enjoy each other's company. And, of course, sometimes it worked out and sometimes it didn't.

He told me about a woman friend of his he'd been in touch with some years earlier. He knew she'd had a few dates with a friend of his we'll call Gordon, and asked her how things were going between them.

"Let me just say this," she said. "You know how they say you can't have too much of a good thing? Well, it just so happens they're wrong."

He asked her what she meant.

"Gordon," she said, "is a real Frenchman, if you get my drift. But that's the only language he speaks, and he doesn't shut up."

"Oh," said Henry.

"Left to his own devices," she said, "he would not stop until his partner was dead, and maybe not even then."

"Oh."

"Now this is a real sweet guy," she said, "and good-looking, and fun to be with. A nice dresser, and good manners. And for the first twenty minutes or so in the feathers, it was clear we were sexually compatible. And then it became clear that we were not."

"Oh."

"A real sweet guy," she said. "But not for me."

Henry thought that was pretty interesting, and added it to his file of sexual lore.

Then not long after he was talking to a male friend who'd had an affair with a prominent actress we'll call Lorraine. "Oh, that's over," the friend told him. "She's a nice woman, enormously talented, and damned attractive. But it's just no good in the sack."

"She doesn't enjoy sex?"

"*Au contraire, mon frere Henri.* She loves it. Can't get enough of it."

"Then—"

"She only wants one thing," the friend confided, "and she doesn't want it to end. She wants to be—how shall I put this?—the *piece de resistance* at the banquet."

"Oh."

"Not that she's not a suitable object for that sort of veneration," he said. "But one doesn't want to spend hours on end kneeling in homage, as it were."

"Hours, eh?"

Henry mulled this new nugget of information, and in the course of the next several days he made two phone calls. The first was to his friend Gordon.

"There's a woman I think you'd really enjoy," he said. "Her name's Lorraine. She's a few years older than you, but I don't see why that should be a problem. Why don't you give her a call, see if the two of you hit it off?"

The second call was to Lorraine, whom he didn't know as well as he knew Gordon, but whom he'd met a few times and felt comfortable calling. "There's a fellow I know named Gordon," he told her, "and I think he's going to call you for a date. I have a strong hunch the two of you would be good together, so why don't you give it a shot and see how it goes?"

And that, said Henry Kane to me, perhaps ten years after those phone calls, is how Gary Morton met Lucille Ball.

I know, I know. It's an outrageous story. And there's no way to confirm it. Wikipedia tells us that the two met while Ball was rehearsing *Wildcat* prior to its Broadway opening, and that a fellow cast member introduced the two of them. And maybe that's what happened, and maybe it's not.

The principals themselves are long gone—I wouldn't dream of recounting the story otherwise—and we're free to believe it or not, as we prefer. I figure it's true, but maybe that's just because I want it to be true. I'll tell you, it adds a certain something to watching reruns of *I Love Lucy*.

Toward the end of our acquaintance, Henry Kane wrote a novel with some sort of espionage element in it. A hardcover house contracted to publish it, and then Something Went Wrong. Someone from one of the intelligence agencies visited Kane's publisher, and the book essentially disappeared.

Now it seems to me that there was once a time when I knew the book's title, and I may even have read it, but on this point my memory is spotty and not to be trusted. I *think* the book was actually published, but can't even be certain of that. What I do recall is that Kane was desperate to know who was responsible for its suppression, and why, and so on. And he couldn't figure out how to learn what he wanted to know.

I suggested he ask himself what his detective, Peter Chambers, would do in such a situation. Or another character, ex-Inspector MacGregor. Figure out who they'd call, and what they'd say, and how they'd solve the puzzle, and then do just that.

I don't think he could see what I was getting at. The characters he wrote could operate in that world, and do so with great panache, but he couldn't even put himself into it in his imagination. He went on railing at Fate, and never did learn who'd put the kibosh on his book, or why.

Toward the end, Henry Kane published a series of erotic suspense novels for Lancer, with titles like *The Shack Job, The Glow Job, The Escort Job,* and *The Tail Job*. I think he ghosted at least one Ellery Queen paperback, and his last novel seems to be *The Little Red Phone,* published in 1982.

It must have been sometime in the early '80s that he died. I had lost track of him by then, and had changed agents myself, so he was long gone by the time I had word of his death. And I'll be damned if I can find out when it was that he died.

Henry Morrison doesn't remember. "All I know is it was a really long time ago," he told me recently. He added that Kane's widow had since died, and that their daughter had moved and his attempts to contact her had been unsuccessful.

I got in touch with a woman I'd met through Kane, an old girlfriend of his, but she too had long-since lost touch with him. She couldn't furnish his date of death, and while she was at it she cast doubt on his official date of birth; she figured he wasn't above taking off a few years, and that he was most likely born not in 1918 but in 1908. And she put me in touch with another old girlfriend of Henry's, with whom I had a perfectly lovely conversation, but she didn't know when he died, either.

You'd think in this age of Google that anybody's date of death would be instantly available, but it'll take someone handier than I with a computer to find it.

But it's pretty clear that he's gone, and I guess somebody said Kaddish for him. I haven't heard any footsteps.

Those Scott Meredith Days

So many of my columns for Mystery Scene *touched on the Scott Meredith agency that I sat down and wrote about those days, and before I knew it one column had stretched to three, with the prospect of a fourth. Scott, of course, was not a writer, he was more of a writer's nightmare—except that in fact he was a writer, had written pulp fiction under several pen names (John Van Praag and Roy Carroll are two I remember) and late in his career produced a labor of love, a lengthy biography of George S. Kaufman. (It gives one very little sense of either the man or his life, but I gather Scott was hugely proud of it.)*

Enough. Here we go:

In the summer of 1956, after my first year at Antioch College, I went to work in the mail room at Pines Publications. One of Antioch's chief attractions was its co-op job program, designed to furnish students with real-world experience in their careers of choice; I wanted to be a writer, so I picked a job at a publishing house.

Pines had a paperback line, Popular Library, and a whole string of magazines and comic books. The job experience was reasonably interesting, but the chance to live on my own in Greenwich Village trumped it. I shared an apartment at 54 Barrow Street with two other Antiochians, and I hung out a lot in Washington Square and the Macdougal Street coffee houses, and one Sunday afternoon I stayed home and set up my typewriter in the kitchen and wrote a story about an amoral kid who lives by his wits, runs a mail-order scam, and like that. End of October I went back to college and took the story with me.

Earlier, I'd read *The Jungle Kids*, a paperback collection of some of Evan Hunter's short stories, packaged to capitalize on the success of *The Blackboard Jungle*. One thing I'd noticed was that most of the stories had appeared in a magazine called *Manhunt*. I'd never seen a copy, but I got the address someplace, most likely *Writers Market*, and I mailed in the story I'd written on Barrow Street.

Now I'd submitted my work before, and indeed had a burgeoning collection of rejection slips taped to the wall of my dorm room. But what I got this time, along with my manuscript, was a note from one Francis X. Lewis, *Manhunt's* editor, saying that the story just sort of trailed off, and needed some kind of a snapper ending. If I could come up with something suitable, I might have a sale.

Damn!

There was a magazine rack in the Yellow Springs drugstore, and, *mirabile dictu*, they carried *Manhunt*. I bought it and read all the stories in it, and I tacked on an O. Henry-type ending which saw the little bastard hoist on his own petard.

Off it went and back it came, with another note from Mr. Lewis, this one rather less heartening. The ending was too pat and predictable, but thanks for trying.

Rats.

A week or so later I got a short note from a man named Scott Meredith, a New York-based literary agent. One of your recent magazine submissions was close, he wrote. This is to express interest in your material.

Well, I already knew that. Close, but no cigar. The enclosed brochure went on to invite me to submit my story for Mr. Meredith's appraisal for a mere $5.

Yeah, right. I tossed it in the trash and forgot about it.

✳   ✳   ✳

In June I went home to Buffalo. I'd decided to go to Cape Cod for the summer, and find some sort of job there instead of filling any of the slots the college had on offer. Night before I drove there, I saw how to fix that story. I drove to the Cape, found an attic room above a barbershop in Hyannis, and right away wrote the story and sent it off to *Manhunt*. I got a job as a dishwasher at Mildred's Chowder House, worked like a dog from four to midnight, and was told to report the following day at eight a.m. I decided against setting my alarm clock, and I never did return to Mildred's joint. (I think I must have been afraid to go back and ask for my pay. "But you quit, you bastard! You didn't come in at eight!" I scored high on IQ tests, but in certain respects I have to say I was a moron.)

For two weeks I stayed in that room, and every day I pounded my typewriter. Three or four days in, I got a note from Francis X. Lewis's assistant. Mr. Lewis was away for the next several weeks, but the assistant had read the story and was pretty sure Mr. Lewis would want to buy it on his return. It was, certainly, under serious consideration.

Gosh . . .

I didn't quite turn out a story a day, but I must have finished, oh, nine stories in two weeks. I remember I aimed one of them at *Boy's Life*, and there was at least one slanted toward *Manhunt*, but that's all I recall about them. I stayed in that attic and lived on Maine sardines, a tin of which cost 15¢. Right before the money ran out, and before I died of sardine poisoning, I took a horrible split-shift job at a fancy resort in Osterville that had me working from 7 a.m. to 9:30 p.m., with a two-hour break in the afternoon. It's good I'd run out of story ideas by then, because the time and energy I had left would limit me to haiku.

Ten days of that was plenty. The summer help had a tradition of quitting the joint, and every few nights another bellhop or bus boy would tie his uniform to a tree and be gone by daybreak. I left at a more conventional hour and drove back to Buffalo, cracked up the car en route, limped home with it, and took a train to New York. I got a room at 105 East 19th Street, at what years later would briefly serve as MWA's headquarters. And I set about looking for a job, and wished Francis X. Lewis would get back from the Catskills or the hospital, wherever he was, and buy my story.

My father had gone to Cornell, and stayed in touch over the years with several of his fraternity brothers. One was Morton Tolleris, who became a prominent judge in New York. Morty had a younger brother named Ralph, and Ralph's wife Beatrice worked at *Time Magazine*. After a few phone calls, I found myself on the phone with Mrs. Tolleris, who was able to offer me a position as a copy boy on *Time*. The pay was $60 a week, and because of their publishing schedule my work week would run from Wednesday through Sunday.

I decided I didn't want the baggage that came with any job I got through a friend of my folks. Suppose I screwed up? Suppose I wanted to quit? So I turned it down, and I'm sure Beatie Tolleris was as relieved as I was, for about the same reason.

A few days later I followed a *New York Times* classified to the offices of Qualified Employment, on West 42nd Street, where I inquired about their listing: Associate Editor, Literary Agency. And there must have been something suggesting that the position was entry-level, or how would I have had the nerve to offer myself up for it?

The chap who interviewed me seemed bemused, and his attitude only deepened as I answered his questions. I wanted to be a writer, I admitted, and had a story under consideration at a national magazine. Which magazine? *Manhunt*, I said. He nodded sagely. Did I like any particular *Manhunt* writers? Well, Evan Hunter. And, uh, Ed McBain.

Next thing I knew I was on the eighteenth floor at 580 Fifth Avenue, where Sidney Meredith sat me down at a desk with a story to read. My task was to write a letter to its author, telling him one of three things—it was great and we're going to market it, it needs fixing and here's how, or it's hopeless and here's why.

The story was "Rattlesnake Cave," and the byline read Ray D. Lester, whom I subsequently learned was the science-fiction writer, Lester Del Rey. He'd deliberately written it to incorporate every structural flaw he could think of, and he'd done his work well. I sat down and read it, and wondered if anyone had ever taken this test and found the story acceptable. (Happened often, I was to learn.)

The story had a frame device, told years after the fact, so we knew the narrator survived, so where was the suspense? It was about snakes, and lots of people, especially women, didn't want to read anything about snakes, ever. And it turned out there weren't any snakes, so the plot was a paper dragon, and the reader felt like an idiot for having been all exercised over nothing. And the regional dialect was spelled phonetically. And—

I didn't have trouble writing a letter that spotlighted these faults. I handed it in to Sid, who looked like a cross between Jack Klugman and Louis Quinn. (Louis Quinn played Roscoe on 77 Sunset Strip. Jack Klugman you know.) He told me I'd hear from them if there was anything to hear. Yeah, right, I thought, and went back to my room on East 19th.

The next day I got a phone call. It was the bemused fellow from Qualified Employment. I had the job.

I went right to work, and that work consisted of doing for the genuine creations of hopeful men and women what I'd done for "Rattlesnake Cave." Across from my desk stood a file cabinet, its top drawer jammed with file folders. Each held a story, no longer accompanied by a check. I'd pull the foremost folder and take it back to my desk.

I'd read the story, and then I'd make a sandwich of a sheet of Scott's letterhead, a sheet of carbon paper, and a sheet of copy paper, and roll all of that into the Remington office model typewriter on my desk. The letter I'd write would start halfway down that first page, and finish close enough to the bottom of a second page so that my subscript would just clear the bottom of the page. (The subscript read SM:lb, suggesting to the world that Scott had dictated his remarks to Lydia Baker or Linda Brown or Lorelei Benatovich, but indicating to anyone in the office that it had originated with me.)

Scott was out of town when I was hired, on his summer vacation, and it was several weeks before he returned. The whole fee report process worked just fine without him. I wrote my reports, and Brother Sid read them and signed Scott's name to them. And off they went.

It generally took a new man a while to get the hang of it, but I hit the ground running, and got out eight reports the first day. I saw right away that I could do this, and it was clear I could learn an enormous amount, and I was grateful for the perverse streak that had saved me from becoming a *Time* copy boy.

After I'd been there a few days, two of my colleagues started a conversation they made sure I overheard. One was Henry Morrison, then handling Foreign Rights, and the other would have been either Jim Bohan, the Pro man, or Ivan Lyons, the Personal Collaboration guy. They were talking about *Manhunt*, and I specifically recall Henry saying something caustic about the magazine. And he roped me into the discussion: Didn't I agree that *Manhunt* was fit for nothing more than lining birdcages?

I hadn't yet said a word about my writing, but how could I resist? "Don't knock *Manhunt*," I said. "They're about to buy a story of mine." And I explained how I was awaiting final word from Francis X. Lewis, as soon as he got back from Bermuda or Boise or Bellevue.

Henry seemed to find this hysterically funny. Or maybe something else had him all giggly. I had a story to read and an author's heart to break, and no time to pay attention.

And why was what I'd said was so amusing?

Here's why:

Manhunt didn't have an editor named Francis X. Lewis, his name on the masthead notwithstanding. His name had recently replaced that of John McCloud, but he didn't exist, either. The magazine was in fact edited by Scott Meredith, and this was one of the agency's deep dark secrets. The clients from whom he bought stories didn't know it, and the other agents he dealt with didn't know it, and God knows I, sitting at my desk and banging away at my typewriter, didn't have a clue.

While I did my work, Henry ducked into the back office, eager to show up the brash new kid. When he and Sid searched the appropriate file, there was my story. Before he left for vacation, Scott had already bought it for inventory; he'd postponed telling me because the magazine was having a not uncharacteristic cash-flow problem.

I learned all this from Sid. "Now your story runs to 2600 words," he said, handing me a sheet of paper. "And ordinarily you'd get $52 for it. But as our client you get a hundred bucks."

I'd sold a story? I was being signed to an agency contract?

I signed the thing. It was just a couple of paragraphs, with a clause stating it would renew automatically unless either party canceled it. For God's sake, it could have included a chattel mortgage on my grandmother and I'd have signed it.

"So the story's sold," I said.

"Oh, yeah," Sid assured me. "You bet."

"My first sale."

"First of many, would be my guess."

"And I'll be getting a hundred dollars."

He shook his head. "You get ninety," he said firmly. "We get ten."

When I started working for Scott Meredith in the summer of 1957, I was an Antioch student on a co-op job. Come October, I was scheduled to return to Yellow Springs, Ohio, and begin my third year as a student at Antioch College.

Of course I hadn't mentioned this when I applied for the job. I was an innocent, God knows, but not a complete moron, and I wanted the job. And I hadn't been there for two weeks before I realized I wanted it a lot more than I wanted a college diploma. I was learning more every day than I could pick up in a month in Yellow Springs.

I said as much to my parents, and told them I wanted to drop out of school. I thought I'd have a fight on my hands, and was surprised

by their ready acquiescence. They'd both always been very supportive of my intention to become a writer, and I think I must have picked
a good time to drop out; I don't think my father was dismayed at the
idea of not having a tuition bill to pay that year.

So I settled in as a fee man—which is what John Dobbin and
I were called. Two kinds of manuscripts turned up in that office,
pro scripts (from professional writers whom Scott represented on a
straight commission basis) and fee scripts (from unestablished writers who paid Scott a fee to read their work). I read the fee scripts,
and wrote fee reports to their authors, and that made me a fee man.

It was, you should pardon the expression, a scam.

Like every viable con game, it looked good to the marks. For the
small sum of $5 (plus another $1 per thousand words, up to a max
of $25 for a full book) they got their efforts read by Scott Meredith
himself. There was a chance (a real one, but much slimmer than they
might have assumed) that Scott would accept their story (or article,
but a good 95% of what came in was fiction) and sell it to somebody.
There was also the chance he'd tell them how to improve it, and *then*
take it to market.

Failing that, he'd tell them at considerable length just what was
wrong with their work. His letter, single-spaced with narrow margins, would begin a third of the way down an impressive piece of
letterhead, and would fill all of a second page as well. (Unless, of
course, they'd written a longer-than-usual manuscript and paid a
larger-than-minimum fee. The fee report for a novel ran clear to the
bottom of page four. Always.)

Now that's a lot of words for what wasn't that much money even
in 1957. So it doesn't sound like a bad deal, does it? So where do I get
off calling it a scam?

Well, for one thing, they weren't getting the considered opinion
of a prominent literary agent, his signature at the bottom of the second page notwithstanding. (They weren't even getting his signature.
Scott never even saw the letters. Brother Sid saw them, and signed
Scott's name to them.)

The ones who read my fee reports were getting the thoughts of a kid who'd just turned nineteen and just sold his first story. Worse yet, they weren't getting my real thoughts, which more often than not were that they couldn't write their names in the dirt with a stick, and should give some serious consideration to dental school.

Of course I didn't tell them anything of the sort. Like everyone else who wrote fee reports, I had nothing but good things to say about the way our fee clients wrote. I always praised the writing and disparaged the plot. Fundamental structural flaws made the story unsaleable, I told them, and thus it couldn't be rewritten, and the author's only recourse was to start fresh with a new story and send it to us—with, of course, a new fee.

But let me walk you through a day at the office . . .

Once I'd walked in at nine or close to it, I'd hang up my jacket. (We wore jackets and ties to the office, but took off the jackets. I don't think it ever occurred to me or to anyone else to show up without a necktie. At one point I acquired a black shirt with a button-down collar, and took to wearing it with a white tie. Henry, visibly embarrassed at the task forced upon him, took me aside on one such sartorial occasion. "Larry," he said, "Scott doesn't remember Mark Hellinger, and he's seen a lot of gangster movies, and, um, well, maybe you could not wear a black shirt and a white tie to the office." "Oh, okay," I said, and the next day I showed up with the black shirt, pairing it this time with a black tie. Nobody ever said a word. And, thinking back, I wonder why we wore ties in the first place, because we had no dealings whatsoever with the public. Nobody ever saw us. Any visitors—and there weren't many—passed directly from the waiting room to the offices in the rear, bypassing our bullpen altogether.)

But I digress.

Once settled in, my first order of business was to walk over to a file cabinet, where the top drawer was filled with fee submissions, arrayed in the order they'd been received. The schedule called for a two-week interval between our receipt of a submission and our reply—long enough so they could believe Scott had been able to give their effort due consideration, but not so long that they'd feel neglected.

Each manuscript was in a file folder, and if the author of the manuscript had had prior dealings with us, all the letters he'd written would be there with it, stapled to carbon copies of our replies. If this was our first crack at him, there'd be just the new story and whatever letter he'd sent along with it.

It didn't take me long to learn to cherish these new people. They were so much easier to reject.

There was a formula, you see, to the rejection letters it was my job to produce. Scott Meredith had written a book, *Writing to Sell*, and in it he'd channeled Aristotle and presented what he called the Plot Skeleton: a strong and sympathetic lead character confronts a problem, his initial struggle to overcome it only deepens his dilemma, and at last through his own admirable efforts he brings things to a satisfactory conclusion.

That's a quick version; in the letters that went out over Scott's signature, we often got half a page out of the plot skeleton. The more space we filled detailing the plot skeleton, the less we were required to say about the story.

And, while the plot was always the ostensible reason for returning the story, it rarely entered into the equation. A writer could copy a plot from Chekhov, and he'd still get the story turned down on the ground that the plot was faulty. (And, on the very rare occasion when someone pointed out that the plot we'd condemned had worked just fine for Irwin Shaw or Damon Runyon or O. Henry, we'd have an answer. We always had an answer.)

Now I'm sure many of the stories I read were inadequately plotted. But I generally knew, before I'd read more than a single page, that I was reading something unpublishable. There were times when I stopped after a page or two, wrote two thirds of my fee report, then scanned the rest of the story to find some particulars to note in explaining why his plot fell short. I made my initial decision and wrote most of my report in the basis of the clunky prose and wooden dialogue, but if I said anything about the writer's style it was to praise it. You're a fine writer, we assured them, one and all. Soon as you come up with a sound plot, the Pulitzer people will be knocking on your door.

Once in a while I provided a suggestion relating to writing technique. I might confide that the writer might do better to have his characters say, for example, rather than assert, interject, comment, and otherwise exhaust the writer's overburdened thesaurus. I was more apt to trot out a tip of that sort with writers who kept coming back for more, who'd already received a full dose of the Plot Skeleton.

(Although that didn't necessarily stop me from refreshing their memories. "Let me take a moment to outline that plot skeleton again, Fred, because I just can't stress it too often . . .")

And every fee report began by thanking the mope for sending the story, and every one ended with the hope that we'd see new work from him soon, with the complimentary closing of All best wishes. My friend and colleague Larry M. Harris (whose name was to become Laurence Janifer, and who deserves a Memory Lane remembrance all his own) summed up our mission in a classic French verse form:

> *Unlike the Ainu and the Manx*
> *We hide the fact that we are vicious,*
> *Starting our letters off with Thanks,*
> *Ending each one with All best wishes.*
> *Further evolved than bugs and fishes,*
> *We are polite to nuts and cranks;*
> *Starting our letters off with Thanks,*
> *Ending each one—O Nature's pranks!*
> *Ending each one with All best wishes.*

I worked Monday to Friday from nine to five, with an hour off for lunch, and I spent those working hours reading stories and returning them to their authors, every last one of whom I encouraged to send us their next effort. I was expected to go through forty stories a week (or their equivalent; a $25 book counted the same as five $5 stories).

For this I was paid $65 a week, plus an additional dollar for each additional story. (Once, just to see what I could do, I took stories home and worked evenings as well. I wound up making $125 that week. I paid $65 a month for my hotel room, so that wasn't bad.) We were all paid in cash; every Friday Scott's brother-in-law, the odious Murray Weller, trotted four blocks down the avenue to Manufacturers Hanover, and we got little brown envelopes holding our after-tax earnings for the week. I never did need to open a bank account, and of course nobody on the planet had a credit card yet.)

I was in the rejection business, and it was quickly made clear that I wasn't expected to enthuse over much of what I read. If I did in fact pass a story to Henry, and if he approved it for marketing, I got the same work credit for writing a three-sentence congratulatory note to the author as I'd get for filling two pages. But if the story came back, a heavy dose of disapproval accompanied it, and I was given to understand that I ought to raise my standards.

For all of that, I did move a very few stories from my desk to Henry's, and for the most part they didn't come back. I can remember two writers by name, whose work I discovered in Scott's slush pile. Charles M. Runyon was one; his first submission was a novel, and it looked to me like a natural for Gold Medal. Henry agreed, and so did Dick Carroll at Gold Medal, and Scott signed Runyon as a straight commission client, so from then on I only got to read his work after it was published.

A little later on a pair of confession stories landed on my desk. The form was one I didn't have much feel for, but I could tell pro caliber work when I saw it. I passed them on to Henry and one sold that afternoon. The other took another whole day. The woman's name was Barbara Bonham, and she too was offered and accepted straight commission representation, and went on to have a solid career.

There were some others, but not many. I wasn't there to find gems on a manure pile. I was there to shovel the stuff back where it came from, and beg for more.

*   *   *

But nobody out in the world realized that. Here was a big-time New York agent reading their stories and giving them tips, all for $5 a pop. Why would he do that? Why, for the reason he stated in his ads and brochures—because he wanted to discover and sign up promising writers for professional representation. After all, he couldn't make money on $5 reading fees, could he?

The hell he couldn't. He was keeping almost $4 for each story, and there were two fee men in the office and one or two more who picked up scripts and worked at home, and the money was good enough for Scott to run a full-page ad every month in *Writers Digest*. And he sent out a lot of direct mail as well. If you submitted an unagented story to *Manhunt*, which he edited, you got a brochure, accompanied by a note from Scott himself: "One of your recent magazine submissions was close. This is to express interest in your material."

Same thing if you sent your story to *Alfred Hitchcock's Mystery Magazine*. Scott had a cozy arrangement with someone in their office, and the empty envelopes that had held submissions came to us every week; Joan, our receptionist, filled her empty hours typing address labels to express interest in their material.

Neat, huh?

Oh, it was a pirate ship, all right, but serving as cabin boy was the best possible job for me. And in the next leg of this hike down Memory Lane I'll tell you what was so great about it.

In my last installment of this seemingly endless experiment in senile recollection, I promised to explain what was so great about working for Scott Meredith. After all, I was putting in forty hours a week reading inferior work and assuring the perpetrators thereof that they were talented, and that their success lay just a few dollars away. Aside from an inside perspective on white-collar moral turpitude, what valuable experience did all of this afford?

Well, I'll tell you. The work itself—reading that garbage, prefatory to encouraging the production of more of it—was the best writing lesson I ever got. There's ever so much more to be learned from bad writing. You can see what's wrong with it.

That's a whole lot easier than seeing what's right with a masterpiece.

I've a feeling that any job that involves reading a vast quantity of amateurish work is a good training ground for anyone with literary aspirations. Back then—and for many years afterward—magazines and book publishers were generally willing to consider unsolicited manuscripts, and the duties of junior editors commonly included reading one's way through the haystack of the slush pile, passing on the occasional needle, and stuffing the rest into those nine-by-twelve self-addressed stamped envelopes.

I'm sure those junior editors gained something from the experience, but far less than was available to me. It was to them what KP was to a soldier—not exactly punishment, but hardly what had moved you to put on the uniform. Slush was a task to be tackled when time permitted, and the slush reader's job was to make the slush pile disappear. If one's time was limited, one might very well return manuscripts unread, without even a glance at the first page.

Even when time was abundant, a slush reader stopped reading as soon as the task became pointless. Once you knew you were going to return a story, why give it any more time? Send it back, and move on to the next.

But I couldn't do that. I too had been engaged to send these stories back where they came from, but instead of a form rejection slip, I had to provide an elaborate explanation of why the story didn't work, along with some insincere flattery designed to encourage future submissions, accompanied to be sure by future reading fees. I didn't have to know a lot about the story to do this, and I didn't need to read it carefully, but I had to skim it sufficiently to bat out a few hundred words about it.

And sometimes, of course, I did have to read the thing attentively, not merely to figure out how to reject it but to determine if rejection was in fact warranted. Although our familiarity with the work bred no end of contempt, not all of our fee clients were entirely without talent. Now and then one came upon a nice turn of phrase, a smattering of engaging dialogue, a promising plot situation. This was hardly ever enough to make the story one I'd pass up the chain to the pro man, but it forced me to pay attention to the thing, noting what worked and what didn't.

A wonderful education. Nowadays only a handful of publications will even look at unagented manuscripts, and I suppose that makes it hard for new writers, but when was it ever easy? The greater loss, I suspect, is to the men and women who might otherwise be employed reading the slush.

Of course I wasn't just reading the fee submissions. I had sold my first story, "You Can't Lose," to *Manhunt*, and while that did not make me a mystery writer overnight, it certainly pointed me in that direction. I'd read a fair amount of crime fiction over the years, but now I began reading with purpose and direction.

There was a shop on Eighth Avenue and 43rd Street that sold back-date magazines, with a huge stock of *Manhunt* and its imitators priced at 2 for 25¢. Even on my wages I could afford to buy every copy I could find, and I took them home and read them cover to cover. I bought used paperbacks, too, and whenever I discovered a writer I liked I would read my way through his works.

I suppose what I was doing was analytical, but I wasn't consciously taking the stories and novels apart to see what made them tick. I was just reading—and by so doing, I suspect I was unconsciously synthesizing all of what I read, so that I could know intuitively what did or didn't make a story.

It might seem like a busman's holiday—read unpublishable crap all day, then read published fiction nights and weekends. But while my reading was not without purpose, there was nothing dogged about it. The writers I enjoyed—too many to mention, or even to recall, but I know that I worked my way through all of Fredric Brown and David Alexander, and a good five years of *Manhunt* stories—were the ones I kept reading. I quit reading the writers I didn't care for.

And, unlike our fee clients, I didn't have to write them a letter when I was done.

When it came to finding new authors to read, all I had to do was pay attention. The office was a small and gossipy place, with half a dozen of us seated at desks. Scott and Sid were in their private offices, and I worked there for several months before I even caught a glimpse of Scott, but plenty of business got done in my hearing. The conversation in the room—and at lunch—was about the business, and about books and writers.

It was an education.

And it was also an apprenticeship, because when I wasn't reading I was apt to be writing. Sid had signed me to an agency contract, and whenever I wrote a story I passed it up to Henry Morrison or Jim Bohan, and with few exceptions the stories I wrote were submitted to magazines. *Manhunt* was hard to hit, but W. W. Scott bought a batch of stories from me for his alternating bimonthlies, *Trapped* and *Guilty*. He paid a cent and a half a word, and the stories he passed on went to Pontiac Publications, where the rate was a cent a word. Just about everything sold sooner or later, and a night's work would bring me $25 or $35 or $50. Many of the pulp stories reissued a few years ago as *One Night Stands & Lost Weekends* were written during those very nights and weekends.

And then there were the assignments. Now and then an editor would call our office; he was up against a deadline and had unfilled pages in his next issue. Or he had an idea and needed someone to write it for him. Could one of Scott's clients deliver the goods, and do so in a hurry?

There was rarely any need to interrupt some client with a phone call, not with a couple of eager writers sitting there in the office. Could I write two thousand words about a really bad Nazi for Ted

Hecht at Stanley Publications? A couple of hours in the library and a stint at the typewriter yielded "Reinhard Heydrich, Blond Beast of the SS." That brought $75, and got Sheldon Lord a byline, as I didn't feel a need to put my own name on the thing.

I went on to write another six or eight pieces for Ted Hecht. They ran in magazines with titles like *All Man* and *Real Men's Stories* and *Man's Bloody Guts*, and sometimes got reprinted a year or two later in another of the company's magazines. Sometimes Hecht called with an idea, which is how I came to write a piece on the 1934 wreck of the SS *Morro Castle*. Sometimes the idea was mine, and that led to "She Doesn't Want You" (about lesbian prostitutes) and "Let's Legalize Marijuana!" (about, duh, legalizing marijuana).

One article I wrote was purportedly a personal experience piece, "by C. O. Jones as told to Sheldon Lord." It became "C. C. Jones" by the time it got into print, suggesting that Hecht or one of his cohorts knew as much gutter Spanish as I did.

One of the more curious assignments came from W. W. Scott, of *Trapped* and *Guilty*. (The magazines were identical, with the same writers producing the same kinds of stories, and the same cover art. Yet *Guilty* consistently outsold its stable mate. Go know.)

W. W. Scott also edited another pair of alternating bimonthlies, *True Medic Stories* and *Real Medic Stories*. These were essentially confession magazines with a medical orientation, and most of the stories involved nurses, even as the magazine's audience was presumed to consist of nurses and nurse wannabes. But at least one story in each issue was told from the point of view of a male doctor, and he wasn't getting enough of those. An assignment came in, and the sum on offer, as I recall, was $200, which was a whole lot better than a cent and a half a word. I grabbed it.

Nowadays, in the world of Google and Wikipedia, I could have done the whole thing without enlisting a partner. But an Antioch friend, Duck Buchanan, was working in the field of medical research, so I proposed that he help me develop a storyline in return for a fourth of the proceeds. Together we dreamed up a plot in which an arrogant surgeon almost loses a patient by overlooking some phenomenon outside his area of expertise.

I don't remember the details, but it seems to me the operation in question was a sigmoid resection, whatever that is. I do recall, word for word, the opening line: "My name is Brad Havilland. I'm forty-two years old, and I'm the best bowel surgeon in the state."

Makes you want to keep reading, doesn't it?

W. W. Scott liked it just fine. I'm not sure which magazine it wound up in, *Real* or *True*. Nor do I recall what title it bore. Duck and I always referred to it as "Pain in the Ass."

I started working for Scott Meredith in August of 1957, and stayed through the following May. Sometime that spring I'd decided to return to Antioch in the fall, and was in fact appointed to edit the college newspaper.

(I'm pretty sure my return owed less to a desire for a degree, or the intellectual stimulation of the classroom, than for fear that I'd be drafted into the army. The same desire to maintain my deferment had already led me to enroll as a matriculated student at Columbia University's School of General Studies, where I signed up for three writing courses—a workshop in the novel, an advanced non-fiction class, and a radio and TV writing course.

(I must have been out of my mind. I stopped going to the radio-TV class almost immediately, when I realized that the textbook would have us following a format—audio on one side of the page, video on the other—that nobody had used in ten or fifteen years. I went to the novel workshop long enough to write thirty pages of a mystery that owed a lot to Fredric Brown's *The Fabulous Clipjoint*, and to realize I didn't know what I was doing, and was well advised to stop doing it. The non-fiction class was written by a terribly nice old fellow who wrote biographies of composers published by Louisiana University Press, and I actually went to that class and turned in work, because it was work I was doing anyway—those "Lemmings Ate My Sister" articles I was knocking out for Ted Hecht. "This is really good work," the professor would say, "but I don't see how you can expect to market it." I was careful not to tell him he'd erred twice in a single sentence; the stuff wasn't good, and I'd already gotten paid for it.

(Wonderful. All day long I read amateur crap at the office, and a couple of nights a week I went up to Columbia and sat there while people read amateur crap out loud. What was I thinking?)

Never mind. For nine or ten months I spent five days a week on the 18th floor at 580 Fifth Avenue, and by the time I left I was a professional writer.

Before I close this installment, I need to offer a correction. Some months ago I attributed "Rattlesnake Cave," the error-ridden story created as a test for job applicants, to the late science fiction writer Lester Del Rey. The byline, transparent enough it would seem, was "Ray D. Lester," and it was common knowledge in the office that Del Rey, an agency client and former employee, had written the piece.

Kate Stine was good enough to point me to an interview Ed Gorman had done with Stephen Marlowe, shortly before Marlowe's death; in it, Marlowe claimed authorship of "Rattlesnake Cave." Did I want to amend my column accordingly?

No, I said. I was sure it was Del Rey, everyone had always known it was Del Rey, and I'd had enough experience with people misremembering the remote past to believe Marlowe had done just that.

So the piece stayed as I wrote it, and when it appeared my friend Barry Malzberg (who knows more about the workings and history of that agency than anyone else ever did, not excepting Scott) put me straight. Steve Marlowe did indeed write it, and the byline was his way of giving Del Rey one in the eye.

I stand corrected. And it may seem a small point, but the damn story has been read by thousands upon thousands of people, including many leading lights of the publishing world. Might as well get it right . . .

*   *   *

When I started writing about my time at SMLA, I saw soon enough that it was going to spill over into two columns. It's now filled three, and there's material I wouldn't want to leave out. Tune in next issue for what I promise you will be the last walk down this particular stretch of Memory Lane.

That's how I concluded the third installment , but I never did get around to the promised fourth. It seemed to me that I'd written all I needed to write about Scott.

Here, though, is a story I can't resist telling. At one point late in the day, Sidney Meredith retired and moved to Florida. After a year or two he came back and paid a call on his brother. Golf wasn't doing it for him, he reported, and you could get sick of all that goddam sunshine, and he'd worked all his life and missed it. So he'd decided to go back to work.

Oh? And what did he plan to do?

"Well, I only did one thing my whole life, so what else do I know? I'm gonna open up shop at a literary agent."

"If that's your decision," Scott said, "I don't suppose I can stop you. But I'll tell you one thing right now. You use the name 'Meredith' and I'll fucking sue you."

His own brother, his partner for what, 40 years? A man who's gone through life saddled with a name Scott chose for him, and God help him if he tries to use it professionally.

Good grief . . .

Not that many friendships develop late in life, but it's been my good fortune to become close in recent years with Barry Malzberg, who spent years in Scott's employ and who wrote brilliantly about him in "Tripping With the Alchemist." (Google will lead you to the essay easily enough, and it's certainly worth your time.)

Barry and I have lunch a couple of times a year, generally at a kosher deli a few blocks from Penn Station, and most of our conversations—like most of our future—is largely in the past. Those Scott Meredith days are a frequent subject. And on one such recent occasion Barry talked at some length on just how bad a human being and how negative a force in the publishing world Scott was.

"And yet," he said, his voice softening, "we owe him everything, you and I. Everything!"

Remembering Al Nussbaum

And now we return to Mystery Scene *for another installment of "The Murders in Memory Lane." If Dashiell Hammett prepared for his literary career as a Pinkerton op, and
Joe Wambaugh as a cop, Al Nussbaum paid his dues on the
other side of the street:*

Sometime in the early eighties Al Nussbaum reported, with a
mixture of disgust and incredulity, that someone had tried to mug
him on his way home the previous night.

"This clown sticks a gun in my face," he said. "I said, 'Get out of
my way, you moron. I just got out of the joint.' "

Al pushed past him, leaving the fellow to go find a more acqui-
escent victim. It's not surprising that his performance was effective;
even in the retelling, his gentle voice hardened and took on an edge
that brooked no argument.

And he came by it honestly. While he wasn't fresh out of prison, it couldn't have been more than ten years or so since he'd been
paroled from Leavenworth after serving eight years of a forty-year
sentence for bank robbery and homicide.

A good number of cops develop literary ambitions, and there was
a time a few years ago when you couldn't get arrested in this town
without hearing about your new acquaintance's novel in progress.
(Now it's screenplays, and TV pitches.)

Few of those books got past the talking stage, and fewer still got finished, and not many were published. But some of them were very good indeed, and if the list began with Joe Wambaugh, it certainly hasn't ended there. And why should we be surprised? Law enforcement, it turns out, is great preparation for a career in crime fiction; as one cop-turned-novelist remarked, the crime part's what you see in the streets, and the fiction's what goes in your case reports.

You would think that a lifetime on the other side of the law would be just as likely to equip one for a second life as a mystery writer. And, to be sure, some powerful crime fiction has been written by chaps with just that sort of firsthand experience. Malcolm Braly's *On the Yard* is arguably the best prison novel ever written, and it wouldn't exist but for the author's having spent half of his first forty years in confinement.

Writing workshops are popular in prison, and if most of the output isn't publishable, well, that's no less true on the outside. On either side of the walls, the writing seems to serve a substantial therapeutic function. And now and then a genuine writer does emerge, and he and we are better for it.

Al was in print and out of the joint by the time I met him in the mid-'70s, but our paths could have crossed earlier. We were both born and raised in Buffalo. He was born four years earlier than I, in 1934, and he left town early enough to get arrested in California in the late 1950s on a weapons charge. That landed him in prison in Chillicothe, Ohio, where he met Bobby Wilcoxson, who'd be his partner in a string of bank robberies.

Al was always a bright guy with a wide range of interests. He played in chess tournaments by mail while locked up in Ohio, and filled his jail time with correspondence courses in locksmithing, gunsmithing, and chemistry. (One wonders at the wisdom of encouraging felons to pursue these interests.) He had some other skills as well; he was a draftsman and a welder, and could both fly and service an airplane.

So he was the brains to Wilcoxson's brawn, and they robbed a batch of banks together. Their last bank job was in Brooklyn, where Wilcoxson shot the bank guard dead.

That was the end of Al's criminal career. And, happily, the beginning of his new life as a writer.

Al was on the lam, and went to ground in Philadelphia. (That's how I heard it, but it may have been somewhere else.) He got a room or small apartment and took care to blend in with his surroundings.

But he didn't have a job to go to, and he worried that this might strike his new neighbors as curious. So he looked for a cover occupation that could explain his presence or absence at all hours. A writer, he thought. I'll pretend to be a writer.

So he went out and bought a typewriter, and now and then during the day he'd pound away at its keys—even as you and I. But that got old in a hurry, and he was resourceful enough to go out and buy himself a tape recorder. Then he made a loop tape of himself typing, and played it whenever he wanted writerly sound effects to seep through his door.

But he felt there might be more to playing a writer than just sounding like one. He needed some tips from an old hand at the game. So one evening he picked up the phone.

Al didn't know any writers. But he'd been a reader for years, and was sufficiently impressed by one book to feel a kinship to its author. The book was *The Name of the Game is Death*, by Dan J. Marlowe, and features a tough and unrepentant professional criminal named Earl Drake. Al was in a position to identify with Drake, and could tell that Marlowe had gotten the character and milieu down right.

He traced Marlowe through his publishers, and called him at home in Royal Oak, Michigan, enthusing over Marlowe's novel and passing himself off as a wannabe writer looking for tips. There were more calls over the weeks and months, and the two men became friends—although Dan didn't yet know Al's real name, or that he was in fact a real-life Earl Drake high up on the FBI's Most Wanted List.

He found out after Al was arrested. That came about back home in Buffalo; Al was visiting his wife and infant daughter, and his mother-in-law ratted him out. (He was captured in the Statler Hilton parking lot after a high-speed chase, and no, I'm not making this up.) The FBI, walking back the cat to make their case, found where Al had been hiding out, checked the phone records, and discovered all these calls to some guy in Michigan. They turned up on Dan Marlowe's doorstep wanting to know why he'd spent so much time on the phone with Al Nussbaum, and Dan didn't know what the hell they were talking about. He'd been helping some young writer who was a big fan of his, he said. And who exactly was this fellow Nussbaum? Dan had to answer a lot of questions before they decided to leave him alone.

A little while later Al got in touch again—this time by mail. By now he'd pled guilty to seven bank robberies and the murder of the bank guard, and was serving forty years in Leavenworth. He wouldn't be eligible for parole until 1971. And he had some time on his hands, and was thinking of trying his hand at something new.

While he served his sentence, Al worked on short fiction. As I heard it, he sent Marlowe his manuscripts, kiting them out of prison; Marlowe wrote back with suggestions for revision, and eventually sent one of Al's stories to *Alfred Hitchcock's Mystery Magazine*.

The relationship wasn't entirely one-sided. Dan had resumed writing about Earl Drake, at Al's suggestion and with his assistance; the expertise he was able to supply didn't hurt a bit. (He'd come by it honestly, is what I was about to write, but on second thought . . .)

After a few books, Dan changed the series; Drake was still Drake, but now he was on the side of the angels, plying his bad-guy skills in the service of the federal government. Some sources indicate that this was Fawcett's idea, that they'd taken over the Parker series (by Donald E. Westlake as Richard Stark) and figured one unrepentant heist man was enough.

Maybe this was indeed the case, but writers do have a lamentable tendency to reform their antisocial protagonists, and maybe readers want it that way; years ago I heard from a reader who informed me that he was quitting my Bernie Rhodenbarr series after the fourth book, *The Burglar Who Studied Spinoza*, because by now Bernie should have seen the error of his ways and gone straight.

More Earl Drake than Parker, Al had indeed seen the error of his ways, and was ready to reform, changing his occupation from bank robber to writer. He kept writing stories and Dan kept marketing them, and when Al became eligible for parole he went before the board with recommendations from editors who'd bought his stories as well as writers Dan had enlisted in his cause. He got out, and spent the rest of his life as a freelance writer, consorting not with fellow criminals but with writers and editors. I don't suppose everyone would consider this a step up, but it worked for him.

But wait, as the TV pitchmen say. There's more.

Dan Marlowe, who's clearly one of the heroes of this story, suffered an absolutely appalling twist of fate. Probably as the result of a stroke, he fell victim in 1977 to a severe form of amnesia of the sort rarely encountered outside the world of soap opera. He forgot who he was, along with all the details of his life to date. It wasn't an ongoing memory loss, in that he had no trouble recalling everything that took place after the stroke. But the past was erased, wiped off the board and forever unrecoverable.

He could still write, lending credence to the folks who insist that what we do isn't really mental in the first place. But he couldn't remember having written, and had to read all his own work as if encountering it for the first time.

Al, fresh out of prison, helped him relearn the world and his place in it. Dan had quit Michigan for California, and Al moved in with him and helped him adjust. Dan wrote a fair amount of softcore porn, much of it under pen names that were anagrams of his own, and the two men did some work in collaboration. Dan never did write more about Earl Drake after his memory loss, and I can see how that would have been daunting; it'd be like taking over a series written by somebody else. Which happens often enough, but it's never quite the same, is it?

Dan resumed writing crime novels and published a bunch of them before his heart gave out in 1986. I haven't read any of them, so I don't know how they compare to his earlier work, though they'd have had to go a long way to match *The Name of the Game is Death*. I had met Dan a couple of times early on, liked him a lot, and was shaken when I heard about his amnesia. He was, no question, one of the good guys.

While I never got to know Al well, I must have met him a dozen times over the years. He was active in MWA and a frequent participant in conventions and symposia, where he was always good company, ever cheerful and sociable. He dealt with his criminal past by being disarmingly open about it; his self-styled business card was a photocopy of his FBI Wanted poster.

I recall one afternoon during Edgar Week when I sat next to him in the audience of some panel discussion, the topic of which I've long since forgotten. One of the panelists was John Ball, best known for *In the Heat of the Night*, who was skilled in aviation, aikido, and rubbing people the wrong way. Ball made a baldly homophobic remark, which brought a spirited rejoinder from Sandra Scoppettone and shifted the direction of the discussion. Al remarked to me that, all things considered, he'd rather spend time with a gay person than a morose one. I chuckled politely, and he was sufficiently encouraged to raise his hand and repeat his observation to the assembly.

A couple of years later he came out, sort of. He was invited as a participant in some mystery colloquium—I wasn't there, and can no longer recall whether it was held aboard a cruise ship or at a resort. Part of his deal was that he could bring someone to share his room, and Al brought Chris Steinbrenner, co-author of *The Encyclopedia of Mystery & Detection*. Neither man seems to have been morose.

If Al never achieved great success, he made enough of a living at his new trade that he was never constrained to resume his old one. He wrote a great many short stories for the crime fiction magazines, along with some episodic TV and young adult novels.

He had a stroke toward the end of his life, walked with a cane after, and seemed frail the last time our paths crossed—at an Edgar dinner, if I remember correctly. I had the feeling that he didn't remember who I was. The stroke may have had something to do with it, or perhaps he was simply unaccustomed to seeing me in a tie and jacket.

He died in 1996, and his work didn't outlive him by much. A short story will turn up now and then in an anthology, but otherwise his work is all out of print. And that's probably to be expected. What's important in this instance, it seems to me, is that the man himself be remembered. The work was secondary to the extraordinary life he led.

Al's daughter, with whom I've had some correspondence, and whom I in fact met at NoirCon in Philadelphia, finds it impossible to believe that her father was homosexual. Well, okay. Perhaps she's right. I'm happy to note her exception, but am not inclined to change what I wrote.

Robert B. Parker

I met Bob Parker eight or ten times over the years. We shared a dais at a luncheon in Boston, appeared together in New York on a program hosted by Lewis Lapham, and ran into each other intermittently at conventions and promotional events.

Just yesterday, as I write these lines, someone tweeted: "When I want to be lied to, I read Robert B. Parker. But when I need someone to tell it like it is, no one beats @Lawrence Block."

It should go without saying that I took that as a compliment. But I don't know that RBP's shade would feel slighted. Parker himself was very clear on his mission; he was writing not Realism but Romance, as noted in the following essay. And the bracing lies of Romance are no less a part of Capital-L Literature than the harsh truths of Realism.

Parker died at his desk, working on a novel, in January of 2010. Some months later, I was invited to contribute an essay on an aspect of the man and his work to a memorial tribute volume, to be published as In Pursuit of Spenser. *Here's the result:*

"They Like the Way It Sounds"

Interviewer: *Why do you think your work is so popular?*
Robert B. Parker: *I dunno. I think people just like the way it sounds.*

That's a wonderfully quotable exchange, and I wish I could be sure I was quoting it correctly. I wasn't there when these words were spoken. It was passed on to me second- or third-hand, but what I heard rang a bell, and I can still hear the echo.

Because I believe he got it right. Why is everything Bob Parker wrote so popular? I think we just like the way it sounds.

Ruth Cavin was a great editor who left us too soon, although not before she'd lived ninety-two years. She stressed the great importance of the writer's voice. It was, Ruth said, as unique as a thumbprint, and the chief factor in the success or failure of a piece of writing. And it was inherent in the writer. You couldn't learn it. You couldn't do a hell of a lot to develop it, or refine it. What you had to do was find it, which was task enough.

And what you found might or might not be worth the effort.

We think of voice more in connection with the performing arts. An actor has a voice, and it amounts to something rather more than pitch and register and tone; it's what makes us listen intently or puts us to sleep.

"I could listen to him read the phone book," we say with admiration.

A musician has a voice. The touch of a particular set of fingers on the keys of a piano, the notes that come out of the bell of a horn—they are individual, and sometimes unmistakably so. You might, if you practice enough, and if you're talented to begin with, play the same sounds Louis Armstrong played. But they won't sound the same.

A singer has a voice. One can almost say that a singer *is* a voice, that anything learned—phrasing, breath control—merely allow the true voice to be heard.

A story, if I may. An aspiring singer went to audition for a great vocal coach. While the last notes died out, the coach sat for a few moments in silence. Then he strode to the window and threw it open, motioning to the singer to join him.

"Listen," he said. "Do you hear the crow?"

"Yes."

"*Caw caw caw.* You hear him?"

"I do."

"The crow," the old man said, "thinks his song is beautiful."

But writing is silent, isn't it? It's an act performed in silence, and its creations are appreciated in a similar silence. (The medium of the audiobook is an exception, in that one reads it not with one's eyes but with one's ears, and there are accordingly two voices involved, those of the writer and the narrator.)

"As silent as a painted ship / Upon a painted ocean," wrote Coleridge, in his own unmistakable voice. We do in fact hear the voice of the writer, all the silence notwithstanding. It falls upon the inner ear. We hear it.

Voice. Isn't it just another word for style?

No.

Different people will define style differently. But I'm writing this, so I get to use my definition. Which goes like this:

Style is that façade a writer erects to conceal his voice.

If Bob Parker wrote a phone book, people would read it.

Well, perhaps I exaggerate. But his voice did have magical

properties. On two separate occasions I picked a book of his off a library shelf, just intending to read a few pages and get an idea of what he was up to in this latest effort.

Fat chance. A few pages? A couple of paragraphs and he had me, and both times I read the book all the way through to the end.

(This would have been less likely had the books had more heft to them, but they were short. There wasn't all that much in the way of incident, nor were all that many words used to tell the tale. In an effort to keep the novels from looking as short as they were, Parker's publishers typically used larger type and wider margins. And they leaded out the text, so that there was often enough space between the lines of a Spenser novel to contain another whole book. The net effect of this typographic enhancement was to make the books even easier to read—as if that were necessary.)

From the opening lines of *The Godwulf Manuscript,* Spenser's first-person voice was a delight to that inner ear. Spenser would become more his own man over time, and less a Back Bay Philip Marlowe, but that's to be expected in a series of any length; the character undergoes a process of self-realization. But Spenser was Spenser from the jump, and his voice didn't change all that much.

And what makes us want to hear it? What makes us listen, even when that mellifluous voice is telling us things we aren't all that eager to hear, even when the story's too thin and the premise too frail and Spenser's task insufficiently challenging?

One ought to be able to take that auctorial voice apart and explain why it does what it does. And maybe someone can do this, but not I. All I can do is say that I think the man got it right:

We like the way it sounds.

I've had occasion to think about Bob Parker's irresistible voice lately, upon the announcement that two writers have been approved by Parker's estate to continue his two most popular series. Ace Atkins will write new books about Spenser, starting next month with

Lullaby, while Michael Brandman's Jesse Stone novel, *Killing the Blues*, came out last fall.

I was surprised when I learned this, but decided on reflection that I had no reason to be. Writers have been taking up the lance of a fallen colleague for a century or more. In today's publishing climate, beset by its own equivalent of global warming, death means never having to say you're done writing. The market dominance of brand-name authors, the glut of books by living authors with acknowledged or unacknowledged "collaborators" or out-and-out ghostwriters, and the pastiche/homage of writers producing prequels and sequels to classic works, all combine to make a continuation of Parker's work an appealing proposition to all concerned.

Though perhaps not quite all. I'm not sure it's such a great deal for the reader.

First, though, there's the question of what Parker himself would think of it. Is he likely to be spinning in his grave at the very idea?

I didn't know the man anywhere near well enough to venture a guess. Ego could tug a writer in either direction; he might be reluctant to see his characters follow him to the grave, or he might be loathe to see others putting words into their mouths.

But any objection from this particular writer would seem to stand on shaky ground. Parker completed *Poodle Springs,* a Philip Marlowe novel that Raymond Chandler left unfinished at his death; later, he wrote a sequel to Chandler's *The Big Sleep,* with the felicitous title *Perchance to Dream.* The man's motives could not have been higher, as he admired Chandler hugely, wrote his doctoral dissertation about him, and quite clearly drew Spenser more from Marlowe than any other source.

And I suppose the books are all right, although one is never in doubt for a moment that another hand than Chandler's is at work here. (In *Perchance,* Parker includes flashback passages from *The Big Sleep,* set off typographically so you'll know they're Chandler's.

This was remarkably daring on his part, I always thought, and not necessarily the best idea he ever had.)

Spinning in his grave? No, probably not.

There are, we should note, some reasons to engage a new author to take over a series. And not just the most obvious one ("We can sell some books! We can make some money!").

I remember questioning the decision to bring out new Nero Wolfe titles after Rex Stout's death. Some years previously, I'd written two mysteries in which the narrator, one Chip Harrison, plays Archie to a road company Nero Wolfe named Leo Haig. John McAleer, Rex Stout's biographer, told me that Stout had indeed been aware of the books, and, like Queen Victoria, was not amused. If Stout bristled at pastiche, how would he feel about downright usurpation of his characters? I figured he could only hate the idea, and I wondered at his family's acquiescence to the proposition.

Then a publisher friend pointed out that it takes a supply of new books to keep the old titles in print. Sales of the Wolfe books had dwindled since their author's death; without new works by a fresh hand, the publisher was inclined to let them go out of print. But if another writer in the person of Robert Goldsborough were to step in, the original books would not only remain in print but would be completely repackaged, with various outside writers commissioned to provide introductions.

All of this sounds itself like a repackaging of *We can sell some books! We can make some money!* and there may well be a self-serving element here. But isn't it safe to presume the author would prefer his own books to remain in print? Wouldn't he want to increase their sales?

Sometimes posthumous sequels work. Sometimes they don't.

And opinions differ. One online reviewer gives high marks to Parker's *Poodle Springs;* a comment follows, decrying the book as a tragedy and saying the publisher should have issued Chandler's four chapters and let it go at that.

I must have read half a dozen of the Oz books when I was a boy, and would have read more if I'd had the chance. While I didn't notice the difference, I remember my mother thought the later books by Ruth Plumly Thompson weren't up to the standard set by L. Frank Baum. (Baum published *The Wonderful Wizard of Oz* in 1900, and the series continues to this day; the most recent entry, licensed by the Baum family, is *Trouble in Oz,* by Sherwood Smith.)

Series continue after the original author's death for the same reason that they become popular in the first place; a reader, having had a pleasant experience, wants to repeat it, wants to renew his acquaintance with a character or characters whose company he's enjoyed. If the author who provided that initial experience is on hand, so much the better. If not, well, too bad; as long as the characters are present, doing what they do, does it really matter who's telling us about it?

It doesn't seem to have mattered much to the young readers who wanted to go back to Oz. Because that's indeed what they wanted, to re-enter that magical realm, and they didn't much care—or notice—who it was that unlocked the door for them. Frank Baum may have created that world, but other writers seemed capable of accessing it, or some acceptable variant thereof. And that's what the books were about, not Baum's perceptions, not his voice.

On the other hand, without departing from the world of juvenile fantasy fiction, try to imagine a later writer taking up the mantle of Lewis Carroll and turning out a third Alice book. It wouldn't astonish me to learn that the attempt has been made, because there's nothing that someone somewhere is not fool enough to try, but aren't you happy you don't have to read it?

I was an impassioned fan of Rex Stout's Nero Wolfe books, and read them all more than once. I read the first of Robert Goldsborough's sequels, and found it troubling. Stout's auctorial voice, and the voice he gave to narrator Archie Goodwin, was more than distinctive; it was to my mind unique, and it had everything to do with the books' success. One wanted to hear that voice, even as one wanted to spend more time in the rooms of that magical brownstone house, and in the presence of those perfectly realized characters.

Goldsborough came to his task more as a fan than an author. He wrote the first book, *Murder in E Minor,* for the private pleasure of his mother, who longed to read more about her favorite characters; it was his own first novel, and wasn't published until 1986, eight years after he'd written it. By 1994 he'd published six more, and that was that. A decade later he began writing books of his own.

As I said, I found *Murder in E Minor* unsettling. It almost felt as though Stout had written it, and the narrator almost sounded like Archie. There was one stunning glitch, in that Archie smoked a cigarette or two in the book's course, and that was about as startling as if Lillian Jackson Braun's Qwilleran were to whip out his pen knife and geld a cat. A few thousand readers called this to the author's attention, and in the books that followed we heard no more of Archie and tobacco.

But the rest, as I said, was almost right. And, naturally enough, Goldsborough improved as he went on. He became a better writer, as one is apt to do with practice, and he also became better at sounding like Stout, and at putting Wolfean words into the mouths of his characters.

It's my impression that members of the Wolfe Pack, that enduring sodality of ardent West 35th Street Irregulars, have varying degrees of enthusiasm for the post-mortem Wolfe books. They did bestow the Nero award on the first book, and surely read the others. The consensus seems to be that they're glad to have these seven further adventures, but do not for a moment confuse them with the genuine article.

I read the first, as I've said, and one or two others. For all I know, they may have been more suspenseful and more strongly plotted than the originals, but I'd never read Rex Stout for plot or suspense. I read, like everybody else, for the pleasure of the writing and the charm of the characters, and Robert Goldsborough was not entirely lacking in those areas. He worked very hard at sounding like Rex Stout, and at letting his narrator sound and act like Archie Goodwin.

Rex Stout, of course, never worked at it. He didn't have to.

And there, I submit, is the problem. Ace Atkins is a fine writer, and at least as gifted in plot construction as Parker himself. (Here's a Spenser plot: 1. A client brings Spenser a problem. 2. Spenser studies the situation and figures it out. 3. Spenser addresses the problem and brings it to a successful conclusion. There's a lot of snappy dialogue and some of the best physical action anyone ever wrote, but those three sentences pretty much cover it in terms of plot.)

I don't know what Ace Atkins has going for him in the way of mimetic ability, but I'm willing to believe he'll do a fine job of sounding like Parker. I gather he's a Parker fan even as Parker was a Chandler fan, and Goldsborough a Rex Stout fan. We can assume he understands Spenser and Hawk and Susan, and will know what words to put in their mouths, and how they'll react to the situations in which he places them.

I can't make all of the same assumptions about Michael Brandman, which whose writing I'm not familiar. As I understand it, his background is TV, and he worked closely with Parker on the adaptations of the Jesse Stone stories for that medium. One might infer that his strengths lie in plot and story construction, but there's no reason he might not be able to provide a reasonable facsimile of the Parker voice.

Here's the thing: No matter how good a job either of these fellows do, no matter how much skill and sensitivity they bring to the table, and no matter how much thought and effort they apply, all they can attempt to provide is an imitation of a genuine original.

I guess there's a place for that sort of thing. Look at all the Elvis impersonators, all the tribute bands.

∗   ∗   ∗

You know, that's enough already. I set out to write about Bob Parker's style and got into a riff on the sequels.

I alluded to this a few paragraphs back, but it can stand elaboration: Nobody ever wrote a better fight scene than Robert B. Parker. Whether the violence is hand-to-hand or includes weapons, whether it's one-on-one or there's a whole crowd on hand, whether it happened the day before yesterday or back in the Old West, the man always got it down brilliantly. He did so with great economy, and spared us the gore and the sadism, but you were right there while it went down, and you could see just what happened and how it happened, and, well, it was breathtaking. I'd read through one of his scenes a couple of times before going on, not because I was going to school (although I probably was) but because I didn't want to let go of the experience.

There's another observation Parker made about his work that has stayed with me ever since I first came upon it. He pointed out that he was not writing realism, that he was in fact writing romance.

Let me capitalize that. He was writing Romance. Not, God help us, in the Harlequin/Silhouette sense, but in the Malory *Morte d'Arthur* sense. And that's why it's perfectly acceptable that Spenser remain the same age forever, that his shining armor remain untarnished, and that, in his affair with Susan, forever wilt he love and she be fair.

It was Parker's special province to write Romance in a realistic style. And that works quite wonderfully, because it tricks us into suspending disbelief to a remarkable extent. We don't strain at gnats, but neither do we refrain from swallowing camels.

Consider the sequence in *Early Autumn,* when Spenser takes Paul Giacomin off to make a man out of him. The physical routine he puts the kid through would flat-out kill him, and Spenser doesn't even give him days off to recover. Parker would have to know as much; he was a weightlifter himself, if perhaps a less diligent one than his hero.

But he writes it this way anyway, because this is Romance, and he makes it work. A realist would teach the kid a couple of basic exercises and start him off with two or three light sets a day of each, and progress would be a gradual thing. That might make just as good reading, but it would be a different sort of book from the one Parker wanted to write.

And one thing he knew was that everything worked out for the best if he wrote the book he wanted to write.

I had my troubles with *Early Autumn*. I'd spent enough time lifting heavy metal objects, and enough days afterward with sore muscles, to find the departure from plausibility hard to take. I've had my problems with Spenser and Stone and Virgil Cole, all of whom may be described as true-blue, uxorious, or pussy-whipped, as you prefer. (The three terms are hardly mutually exclusive.)

So? I was never the Ideal Reader for Parker's work, and God knows he got along fine without me. But I did read almost all of the books, and not because of the stories he chose to tell or the characters who peopled them.

I just kind of liked the way they sounded.

And I liked and respected the man. Let's not leave that out.

I don't think our paths crossed more than eight or ten times, and we never came close to sitting down for a heart-to-heart. There were a couple of dinners where we were both on the dais, a couple of book biz events that threw us together.

Once, I think at a Left Coast Crime conference in Scottsdale, Bob was doing a one-man act in a large room that was predictably packed. He said he wasn't comfortable preparing talks, but would do a Q&A—and, not surprisingly, turned out to be very good at it.

Somebody asked him which of his own books was his favorite. "Gee, I don't know," he said. "Once they're done I never look at them." I was all the way in the rear, but I guess he'd spotted me. "How about you, Larry?" he called out. "Do you ever read your own work?"

"I read nothing else," I said.

Lord, that was satisfying. You have to love a guy who floats one belt-high across the plate like that, and does so on the one day in twenty when you're quick enough to get your bat on it.

I was a bad choice to write this piece, and would have passed if I felt I could. But, if my feelings for the work are mixed, those for the man are not. I was in fact honored to be invited to this particular clambake, and simply could not say no.

Edgar Allan Poe

No, I never knew the man. It's true I've been around a long time, but the curious little man who might be called the Father of Genre Fiction had left the scene before I appeared on it.

Still, I feel a connection. At a Mystery Writers of America event marking the restoration of Poe's house in the Bronx, I gave a spirited reading of "The Bells," and few who were there will soon forget it, much as they might wish they could.

Here, then, are three short pieces on the Master Himself. The first was written as the introduction of an MWA anthology, of which I was the nominal editor. (My "editing" consisted of supplying the introduction.)

"It All Started With Poe"

If you want to blame someone, try Edgar Allan Poe. He's the guy who started it.

Or did he? Maybe this would be a good place to mention Mauritz Christopher Hansen. A Norwegian writer, born 1794, died 1842. In 1827 he published "Novellen" ("The Short Story"), an armchair detective mystery concerning a case of murder and revenge. So he got there first, well ahead of Poe's "The Murders in the Rue Morgue," but he wrote in Norwegian, with the result that nobody ever heard of him. Well, nobody outside of Norway. Matter of fact, you *wouldn't have heard of him either, if your Norwegian friend Nils Nordberg hadn't told you about him.*

Memo: Email Nils, suggest he translate Hansen for Ellery Queen's Mystery Magazine. *Either "Novellen" or his short novel, "Mordet paa Maskinbygger Roolfsen" ("The Murder of Engineer Roolfsen").*

Still, what did Hansen start? If a tree falls in a forest, and only Norwegians can hear it, it's not exactly the shot heard round the world, is it? Poe started it, but who cares? I mean, how many lame introductions have already trotted out poor old Poe?

Think of something else, will you?

It's a rare pleasure to introduce *Blood on Their Hands*, the latest collection of stories by members of Mystery Writers of America. MWA, as its name implies, is an organization of American mystery writers who . . .

Duh. Who write American mysteries, and they hammer them out one inspired word at a time, even as you are attempting to pound out this introduction. Do you really want to bore everybody with the history of the organization, explaining how a handful of hacks and drunks banded together, adopted the motto "Crime Does Not Pay . . . Enough!" and, when they weren't busy hacking and drinking, got on with the serious business of giving one another awards. You can fill space this way, but do you want to?

It's a fine organization, MWA, and virtually every crime writer of distinction is proud to be a member of it. But everybody knows that, so why waste their time telling them?

Start over.

The stories you are about to read . . .

. . . are guaranteed to cure cancer, ensure world peace, and

solve once and for all the problem of global warming. They're ex-cellent stories, as it happens, but what can you say about them that will make them any more of a treat than they already are?

It's my great pleasure . . .

Yeah, I can tell. You know something? You've done too many introductions, my friend, and you're getting worse at it, and you were never that good in the first place. You always used to start out by decrying the whole idea of an introduction, urging readers to get on with it and read the stories themselves, and now you seem determined to prove how dopey an introduction can be by mumbling and stammering and generally behaving like an idiot.
You promised them an intro. Write it, will you? Just spit it out!

It all started with Poe.

Great, just brilliant. "It all started with Poe." And here's where it stops.

In 2008, Michael Connelly invited me to contribute an essay on Poe to In the Shadow of the Master, *an MWA-sponsored volume which would combine a selection of the man's tales with a group of new pieces about the man, all to be published the following year in celebration of the bicentennial of Poe's birth.*
Thus the following:

The Curse of Amontillado

I knew I wanted an Edgar Allan Poe award back in 1961, when my good friend Don Westlake failed to win one.

He'd just published *The Mercenaries,* and it was nominated for an Edgar for best first mystery. Someone else took home the statu-ette (for what was in fact a first mystery by a veteran science-fiction writer, which made it eligible under the letter if not the spirit of the rule) and we all assured Don that it was honor enough to be nominated, and he pretended to believe us. We don't need to feel sorry for the man; he has a whole shelf full of those porcelain busts, plus a sheaf of nominations. Anyway, this isn't about him.

It's about me.

I began publishing paperback original crime novels in 1961, and hardcovers a few years later. And, while I can't say I was obsessed with the idea of winning an Edgar, I had my hopes. One book I published in the mid-'70s, under a pen name (Chip Harrison) which was also the name of the book's narrator, was dedicated "To Barbara Bonham, Newgate Callendar, John Dickson Carr, and the Edgar Awards Committee of the Mystery Writers of America."

Barbara Bonham was the chief fiction reviewer for *Publishers Weekly*. Newgate Callendar was music critic Harold Schonberg's pen name for his Crime column in the *New York Times Book Review*. And John Dickson Carr, master of the locked room, reviewed mysteries for *EQMM*.

I was shameless, and to no avail. Well, not much avail, anyway. The book got a mention in the Callendar column, where its dedication was quoted and its literary merits overlooked. Carr and Bonham paid no attention, and when Edgar time rolled around, Chip Harrison was out in the cold.

But a year or so later one of my Matthew Scudder novels, *Time to Murder and Create*, picked up a nomination for Best Paperback Original. I went to the dinner somehow convinced I was going to win, and I didn't. Someone else did. I sat there stunned, barely able to assure people that it was honor enough merely to be nominated.

A couple of years later, I was nominated again, this time for *Eight Million Ways to Die*, shortlisted for Best novel. "Honor enough to be nominated," I muttered, and went home.

It took years for me to realize what was holding me back. It was, quite simply, a curse.

The curse of Amontillado.

＊　　＊　　＊

I realized the precise dimensions of this only recently, when Charles Ardai was editing an early pseudonymous book of mine for his Hard Case Crime imprint. He pointed out that I'd referred to "The Cask of Amontillado" as having been written by Robert Louis Stevenson. Gently he asked if my attributing Poe's story to Stevenson was deliberate, indicating something subtle about the character who'd made the error.

The mistake, I replied, was not the character's but my own, and he should by all means correct it.

And not a moment too soon. Because it was clearly responsible for a long train of misfortunes.

This misattribution, I must confess, was not an isolated slip-of-the-keyboard confined to a single forgettable book. While that may have been the only time I publicly handed Poe's classic tale to Stevenson, I'd been confused about its authorship ever since I read the story. Which, if memory serves (and you can already tell what ill service it tends to provide), came about in the seventh grade, some fifty-seven years ago.

One of our textbooks in English class was a small blue volume of short stories, and one of the stories was "The Cask of Amontillado," and one was something by Stevenson. (I seemed to recall the title of the Stevenson story as "The Master of Ballantrae," but that's impossible, because it's a novel. So I don't know what the Stevenson story may have been, and, God forgive me, I don't care, either.)

I don't know what else I may have retained from the seventh grade, but one thing I held onto was that story, "The Cask of Amontillado."

"For the love of God, Montresor!"
"Yes," I said, "for the love of God."

They don't write 'em like that anymore, and I knew that even then. But somehow I got it into my head that the author's initials were R.L.S., not E.A.P. Now and then it would come up in conversation, and someone would say I meant Poe, didn't I? And I'd say yes, of course, and stand corrected—but not for long, because my memory remained inexplicably loyal to Stevenson.

Well, really. Where did I get off looking to win an Edgar? If the Red Sox could go that long without a World Series win, just because their cheapjack owner let go of Babe Ruth, well, really, what did I expect?

And then, of course, everything changed.

Because I started keeping company with a young woman named Lynne Wood.

And why, you may ask, should that serve to lift the curse of Amontillado? Perhaps the answer will begin to become clear when I tell you that the maiden name of Ms. Wood's mother was Emilie Poe.

She was not the first person I'd met with that surname. Back in the eighth grade, a mere year after I'd read about Montresor and the ill-named Fortunato, I had a classmate named William Poe. His family had just moved north from Alabama, and that made him an exotic creature indeed at P.S. 66 in Buffalo, New York. We teased him relentlessly about his accent—and I wouldn't be surprised if that helped reinforce the curse, now that I think about it. I don't know that anyone asked if he was related to *the* Poe, but he very likely would have answered that he was, because they all are. The Poes, that is.

Of course none of them are direct descendants of Edgar Allan, because the poor fellow had no living issue. But he has plenty of collateral descendants, and one of them was named Emilie, and she had a daughter named Lynne.

Reader, I married her.

And within the year my short story, "By the Dawn's Early Light," was nominated for an Edgar. Lynne and I attended what I'd come to term the Always-A-Bridesmaid dinner, and this time I went home with a porcelain bust of my bride's great-great-great-etc. uncle.

It has, I blush to admit, been joined by others in the years that followed. Coincidence?

I don't think so.

That might well be enough, but a couple of years later the editor of the MWA Annual, to be distributed at the Edgar Awards Banquet, asked for a piece on what the ways in which winning an Edgar had changed my life. (Several of us were asked to write on this woefully self-congratulatory topic. I didn't read the others' efforts, and can only hope they didn't read mine.)

It repeats much of the previous piece, and I've thought about leaving it out, but here it is. If it has a virtue, it's brevity:

The Edgar and I

Well, I always wanted one.

Back in 1960, my good friend Don Westlake published his first novel, *The Mercenaries,* and the following spring it was nominated for an Edgar. He and his then-wife attended the awards dinner, and I and my then-wife helped fill out the table. All four of us—Don most of all—were disheartened when someone else won, and I went home thinking how nice it would be some day to win one of those things myself.

In 1975, Fawcett published *The Topless Tulip Caper,* with Chip Harrison serving as the lead character and putative author. The book was dedicated quite shamelessly "to Barbara Bannon, John Dickson Carr, Newgate Callendar, and the Edgar Awards Committee of the Mystery Writers of America." At the time, Barbara Bannon provided the greater portion of *Publishers Weekly's* fiction reviews, while Messrs. Carr and Callendar reviewed for *EQMM* and the *New York Times Book Review* respectively. The dedication did induce Harold Schonberg (aka Newgate Callendar) to mention the book, but Carr and Bannon were able to resist, and so was MWA.

But in 1977 Dell published *Time to Murder and Create,* and in the spring of 1978 I found myself up for an Edgar for Best Paperback Mystery. I went to the dinner, and for some inexplicable reason I just *knew* I was going to win. I don't know what had me convinced. I can't remember what other books were nominated, but know I'd never read any of them, so what made me assume the judges would like my book better? Never mind. All I know is I sat through the first few courses running through my acceptance remarks in my mind, trying to strike a balance between the confidence of an established artist and the humility of a saint.

Then they read somebody else's name, and gave this usurper the little statue. I couldn't believe it. How the hell did that happen?

A couple of years later I was up for best novel, with *Eight Million Ways to Die.* I figured I had a chance, but knew I was bucking stiff competition, including Westlake's *Kahawa* and Dutch Leonard's *LaBrava.* Well, I didn't win that year, and neither did Don or Dutch.

I was nominated again a few years later for a short story, "By the Dawn's Early Light." By this time I'd taken to referring to the evening as the Always-A-Bridesmaid Dinner. But this time, remarkably, Edgar went home with me.

And he's done so four times since then—twice for short stories, once for Best Novel, and once when MWA, beaten into submission by my stubborn persistence, made me a Grand Master. So there's a little grouping on a shelf, the Poe Quints, if you will, and it brightens my spirits to see them.

And how have they changed my life?

Well, that's hard to say. It has, to be sure, assuaged the bitter disappointment that not winning had engendered. "It's satisfying enough merely to be nominated" is something everybody says, and maybe someone has spoken these words and meant every one of them, but I wouldn't count on it. Being nominated is thrilling in prospect, when it hasn't happened to you, but once you've been nominated then winning is all that seems to matter.

"It's enough merely to play in the World Series." (Or the Super

Bowl, or the finals in the local shuffleboard tournament.) "Winning's not all that important." Did anyone ever say that? I didn't think so.

What I've come to realize, though, is that while being nominated is never enough, the work itself *is* enough—with or without awards or nominations. When all is said and done, or even when it isn't, the work alone is the only thing that really matters.

That said, it's hard to say how the Edgar has made a difference for me. In recent years publishers have come to regard it as important, and worth trumpeting on covers and in press releases. (It was not ever thus, incidentally. Half a century ago, when perhaps a hundred people showed up for MWA's annual awards dinner, an Edgar didn't mean much outside the literary backwater of mystery fiction. All in all, Rodney Dangerfield got more respect.)

So I don't really know how my Edgars have changed my life. Have they brought me more dollars? More readers? More respect? Have they led reviewers and store buyers to take my work more seriously?

Well, I can't see how they've hurt.

And have they perhaps made *me* more conscious of my potential to produce good work, and thus induced me to dig deeper and work harder?

I suppose that's possible.

But there they stand on the shelf, all five of them, looking for all the world like an overgrown barbershop quartet, about to break into "Sweet Adeline."

Gosh. Don't they look fine?

Spider Robinson

I wrote this as the introduction to a collection of Spider Robinson's essays. Several years later he wrote the most remarkable introduction to a limited edition of my novel, Random Walk. *Man, did I ever come out ahead on that one—and in my intro, you'll notice, I talk about another time I came out ahead of the game.*

If memory serves (and, increasingly, it only stands and waits) I first met Spider Robinson somewhere in cyberspace in 1999. He emailed me to find out if I'd provide a blurb for a book of his, and I emailed back to say that I wouldn't.

That probably doesn't sound like much of a foundation on which to build a friendship. Well, a lot you know.

Spider prefaced his request with an apology for making it, and I explained my refusal as a matter of policy, and we said a number of nice things about each other's work, and placed one another on our respective mailing lists. And, let me tell you, I came out way ahead on that deal. What Spider got was a slew of tour schedules, book offers, and other drivel from the LB Institute for Perpetual Self-Promotion. What I got was an advance peek at each of Spider's columns, always accompanied by a note advising me to let him know if I wanted to be spared further installments thereof.

Why on earth would I want to get off that list? I have never for one moment entertained such a notion. *Au contraire, mon frere.* What I did almost immediately was open a Spider Robinson folder and save each column as soon as I'd finished reading it. I didn't want to let go of them. Now I suppose I could delete the folder, as I've got the columns (including a couple I somehow missed) right here in book form. But I think I'll let them have hard-drive space as well.

The man's entertaining, provocative, and of a wholly original turn of mind and phrase. Moreover, he's evidently incapable of writing an awkward sentence. (Oh, I suppose he could do it if he tried. But not if he didn't.)

But you know all that.

And there's the real challenge in writing this introduction. I am, inevitably, preaching to the choir, because who else is going to show up? However heroic an effort the publisher might make (and, for a small press, every effort is heroic), the likelihood of the book being plucked off the shelf by someone unacquainted with Spider's work is as remote as Tierra del Fuego and as unlikely as Michael Jackson. (Yes, I know, people do get to TdF—I've been there myself—and MJ does exist, albeit in a parallel universe.)

In point of fact, the members of this volume's audience are very likely better versed and more deeply steeped than I in the man's work. I've read (and have now reread) the columns, and I've read a couple of the Callahan books, but many of you have read ALL of the Callahan books, and read them over and over and over, and can (and, alas, do) quote them verbatim, and at some length, upon the slightest provocation.

All things considered (well, at least as many of them as I can think of), I can't flatter myself into believing that anything I can write here will induce anyone to buy the book, or render the experience of owning and reading it one whit more pleasurable than it would be without my participation. Saying things about the columns is pointless. They're not "The Waste Land," for God's sake. You don't have to tunnel like a badger to root out their hidden meanings. And a good thing, too.

We don't need no steenkin' badgers.

*   *   *

Still, I have to say something. I am, after all, getting paid for these words, so it's my job to furnish a reasonable number of them. Pointing out the excellent qualities of the man and his work does seem beside the point, but what else am I qualified to do?

Let me see. I've only met the man once, if you rule out encounters through the email ether, and the no less intimate contact two human beings achieve through sympathetic reading of one another's work. In July of 2001, my wife and I flew to Vancouver, where we were to embark on a two-week Alaska cruise on the *World Discoverer*. Spider and his wife met us, and we walked around downtown Vancouver a bit, and had lunch somewhere, and found that we liked each other as well face to face as we had at a distance.

Later, we found we had an interesting friend in common, a dear man and brilliant writer named Larry Janifer. I had known Larry back in the late '50s, and lost touch with him for years; Spider knew him later in life. Larry moved to Australia, where I was curiously unable to see him because his phone was always busy because he was always on-line. Every few hours he would phone and leave a message at my hotel, and I would call back, and his line would be busy again.

Then health problems led Larry to move back to the States, where he died. And, now that I think about it, I'm not sure just what that has to do with anything, but Larry played a formative role in my career and, I gather, in Spider's, and he's too little remembered these days, so I figured this was a good place to mention him.

I tried to dedicate a book to Spider once.

The book was *Tanner's Tiger,* and it hadn't borne any dedication when Gold Medal published it in 1968. A few years ago Subterranean Press brought out a handsome hardcover first edition, and I seized the opportunity to dedicate it to someone, and picked Spider, because the book takes place in Canada, and so, generally, does Spider.

When my author's copies arrived, I plucked one off the stack, ready to inscribe it to the dedicatee.

No dedication.

Well, these things happen. As far as I'm concerned, *Tanner's Tiger* is dedicated to Spider Robinson, whether it says so or not.

And that, Dear Reader, is as much as you need to hear from me. Turn your attention, I entreat you, to the essays that follow. And if you can get past the "My crows . . ." groaner in the first chapter, you can handle anything.

Mickey Spillane

When Dutton reissued some novels of Mickey Spillane's in a pair of omnibus volumes, I was asked to write an intro- duction for one of them. I liked Mickey, and the year MWA made him a Grand Master was also the year I wore a Ro- man collar to the Edgar dinner. (I don't remember why, but a lot of doormen were more respectful than usual to me that night.) Mickey loved my outfit, and we took a picture together.

Here's what I wrote about him:

I don't know what the hell Mickey Spillane needs with an in- troduction. He certainly didn't get one when the first Dutton hard- covers and Signet paperbacks appeared half a century ago. There were no prefatory remarks by the author, no back cover blurbs by admiring colleagues, no pithy extracts from rave reviews. (There may have been some admiring colleagues around, but, as I recall, there weren't a whole lot of rave reviews.)

Nobody had to introduce you to Mike Hammer. You picked up a book and opened it, and he introduced himself.

Like this, in *One Lonely Night*:

> "Nobody ever walked across the bridge, not on a night like this. The rain was misty enough to be almost fog-like, a cold gray curtain that separated me from the pale ovals of white that were faces locked behind the steamed-up windows of the cars

that hissed by. Even the brilliance that was Manhattan by night was reduced to a few sleepy yellow lights off in the distance.

"Some place over there I had left my car and started walking, burying my head in the collar of my raincoat, with the night pulled in around me like a blanket. I walked and I smoked and I flipped the butts ahead of me and watched them arch to the pavement and fizzle out with one last wink. If there was life behind the windows of the buildings on either side of me, I didn't notice it. The street was mine, all mine. They gave it to me gladly and wondered why I wanted it so nice and all alone."

Or, if that's too hard to get into, try *The Big Kill*:

"Two drunks with a nickel between them were arguing over what to play on the juke box until a tomato in a dress that was too tight a year ago pushed the key that started off something noisy and hot. One of the drunks wanted to dance and she gave him a shove. So he danced with the other drunk.

"She saw me sitting there with my stool tipped back against the cigarette machine and change of a fin on the bar, decided I could afford a wet evening for two and walked over with her hips waving hello.

" 'You're new around here, ain't ya?'

" 'Nah. I've been here since six o'clock.'

" 'Buy me a drink?' She crowded in next to me, seeing how much of herself she could plaster against my legs.

" 'No.' It caught her by surprise and she quit rubbing.

" 'Don't gentlemen usually buy ladies a drink?'

" 'I'm not a gentleman, kid.'

" 'I ain't a lady either so buy me a drink.'

"So I bought her a drink . . ."

Here's how he does it in *Kiss Me, Deadly*:

"All I saw was the dame standing there in the glare of the

headlights waving her arms like a huge puppet and the curse I spit out filled the car and my own ears. I wrenched the wheel over, felt the rear end start to slide, brought it out with a splash of power and almost ran up the side of the cliff as the car fishtailed. The brakes bit in, gouging a furrow in the shoulder, then jumped to the pavement and held.

"Somehow I had managed a sweeping curve around the babe. For a few seconds she had been living on stolen time because instead of getting out of the way she had tried to stay in the beam of the headlights. I sat there and let myself shake. The butt that had fallen out of my mouth had burned a hole in the leg of my pants and I flipped it out the window. The stink of burned rubber and brake lining hung in the air like smoke and I was thinking of every damn thing I ever wanted to say to a harebrained woman so I could have it ready when I got my hands on her.

"That was as far as I got. She was there in the car beside me, the door slammed shut and she said, 'Thanks, mister.' "

You see what I mean? What you want to do now is keep reading, not sit around while some clown explains why what you just read was gripping. I have to write this crap—I'm getting paid, and I have to give the people something for their money—but you don't have to read it, and I don't see why you would want to. Skip past these ill-chosen words of mine, shake hands with Mike Hammer, and enjoy yourself.

Still with me, eh? Oh, well. Have it your own way.

Hammett and Hemingway and plain-spoken, hardboiled fiction were born in the Prohibition Era in the aftermath of the First World War. Twenty years and another war later, Mickey Spillane wrote a series of books that grabbed a new generation of readers. Spillane was a vet, and it was vets and their kid brothers who constituted his eager audience.

Spillane's books were different, though no one could tell you exactly how. The action was slam-bang, but that was true of pulp fiction written thirty years earlier. His hero was blunt and violent, given to taking the law into his own hands, but no more so than Carroll John Daly's Race Williams, to mention one of many. There was sexual content, too, but it's hard nowadays to imagine that the decorous erotic episodes in these books could have inflamed a generation of adolescent males. There were people who denounced Spillane for writing pornography, and you've got to wonder what they were thinking of.

If I were an academic I could spin out a hundred thousand words in an attempt to explain what makes Spillane Spillane, but I'm not, and we can all be thankful for that. I'll boil it all down to two words:

Comic books.

Before he wrote novels, Mickey Spillane wrote for the comic books. His first prose fiction consisted of a slew of one- and two-page stories for the comics, and his hero, Mike Hammer, was originally intended as a comic-strip hero. The fast cuts, the in-your-face immediacy, and the clear-cut, no-shades-of-gray, good v. evil story lines of the Mike Hammer books come straight out of the comic book world.

Mickey Spillane was writing something new—comic books for grown-ups.

The new generation of readers who embraced Spillane had read comic books before they read novels. They were used to the pace, the frame-by-frame rhythm. And they took to Mike Hammer like a duck to a pool of dark red blood shimmering in the sickly yellow light of the streetlamp . . .

Sorry. I got carried away there for a moment.

Mickey died in 2006, and a few years later I wrote about him for my "Murders in Memory Lane" column in Mystery Scene.

He was born Frank Morrison Spillane in Brooklyn, New York, on March 9, 1918, and grew up across the river in Elizabeth, New

Jersey. He went to college briefly (and, I have to say, improbably) in Hays, Kansas, and worked as a lifeguard and a circus trampoline artist, among other things, before enlisting in the Army Air Corps the day after the attack on Pearl Harbor.

But you don't need me to tell you that. You can do what I did and find it on Wikipedia.

And therein lies my present dilemma. I began writing these columns in order to share some personal recollections of writer friends who had passed on, stories which were mine—and sometimes mine alone—to tell. I haven't been doing this all that long, and already I find myself running out of dead friends.

Which is fine with me, as I'd always rather have a living friend than a subject for a column. But this month it leaves me looking to write something about a man I didn't know all that well.

I certainly didn't know him nearly as well, or for nearly as long, as Max Allan Collins, who idolized Mickey Spillane the writer and became a very close friend of Mickey Spillane the man; since Mickey's death in 2006, Al has served as Mickey's literary executor, skillfully and sensitively preparing some unfinished manuscripts for publication, starting with a final Mike Hammer novel, *The Goliath Bone,* in 2008. (Since then we've had *The Big Bang,* with *Kiss Her Goodbye* and *The Consummata* due this year.)

Al's recollections of Mickey would very likely fill a book, and I can only hope that someday they do just that. But perhaps mine, fleshed out with some thoughts and observations, may at least fill a column.

My favorite Mickey Spillane story is one I heard a year or two before I ever met the man. More than twenty years ago, several crime novelists were invited to appear for a radio panel discussion of their craft. I wasn't one of them, but Donald E. Westlake was, and it was he who told me the story. Whoever the panelists were, they nattered back and forth until their hour was up, and then, when they were off the air, Spillane said, "You know what? We never talked about money."

If I remember correctly, Long John Nebel was the host. Whoever the lucky fellow was, he winced at this, and steeled himself to explain to the creator of Mike Hammer that there was no money budgeted to pay the panelists.

But that wasn't what Mickey was getting at.

"We didn't talk about money," he said, "and money's very important. Let me give you an example. Back when we first moved down to South Carolina, I just relaxed and took it easy for a while, and every now and then it would occur to me that it would be fun to write a story. But I didn't have any ideas. I would take long walks on the beach, I would sit and think, but I could never manage to come up with an idea.

"Then one day I got a call from my accountant. 'Mickey,' he said, 'it's not desperate or anything, but the money's starting to run low. It might be a good idea to generate some income.'

"So I thanked him and hung up the phone, and I took a walk on the beach, and *bang!* Just like that, I started getting ideas!"

Mickey wasn't being cynical. What he was doing, it seems to me, was telling a plain truth about the mechanics of artistic creativity. Necessity, for the writer as for anyone else, is very much the mother of invention. We get ideas because we feel a need for ideas, and when that need vanishes the well of ideas goes dry—until it's needed once again.

This is not to say that it's only money that makes the mare go. When I began writing I certainly hoped to get paid for it, but self-expression and ego gratification were far more powerful motivators. And I'd guess that was true at least in part for Mickey—for a certain number of years. And then it wasn't.

Mickey published *I, the Jury*, in 1947. It didn't do much as a Dutton hardcover, but sold like crazy once it went into paperback. Then he wrote and published six more novels between 1950 and 1952—*My Gun Is Quick, Vengeance Is Mine!, The Big Kill, The Long Wait, One Lonely Night,* and *Kiss Me, Deadly.* All but *The Long Wait* feature

Mike Hammer, and it's these seven books that (at least as of 1980) were among the fifteen bestselling American novels of all time.

Mickey would tell you that he wrote the books for money, and I'm sure he did. But those first seven books had a drive and energy he never entirely recaptured in later years, even as his later books never matched them in popularity. I think it's safe to say they came out of his inner self in a way that later books did not, that he needed to write them for reasons having little to do with dollars and cents.

Then he moved to Murrells Inlet, South Carolina, and stopped writing. Then the accountant called and he started in again.

I was probably in Mickey's company half a dozen times over the last ten or twelve years of his life. On several of those occasions I heard him say the same thing: "I'm not an author. I'm a writer."

I wanted to ask him what the hell he meant. The distinction he drew was clearly not out of a dictionary. I knew what he was getting at, that *author* implied some sort of lah-di-dah ivory-tower full-of-oneself attitude, while a *writer* could be free of pretense, a solid regular-guy craftsman producing something for ordinary folks to read. Velvet collar versus blue collar, if you will.

Well, okay. The guy was Mickey Spillane, so I figured he could get away with saying something like that if he wanted to. But there was a chip-on-the-shoulder thuggishness to it that I found off-putting. It seemed a curious attitude for a guy who made a living making up stories and writing them down.

Maybe the critics' barbs hurt, and this was his response.

Then a couple of weeks ago I found a quote from Colette, who was hardly a sterile academician herself, and I just loved the way it worked in juxtaposition with Mickey's oft-repeated line. So for a while I used them both as a subscript for my email correspondence, and here's how they look together:

"I'm not an author. I'm a writer."
—Mickey Spillane
"Sit down and put down everything that comes into your head and then you're a writer. But an author is one who can judge his own stuff's worth, without pity, and destroy most of it."
—Colette

I don't know that I read all of Mickey's first seven books, but it's possible. I was in high school when the Signet paperbacks came out, and that's when I read them.

I thought they were okay. At the time a lot of my reading was in search of sexual excitement and information, and Mickey Spillane had a reputation in that area, but even then it seemed a stretch to call the work erotic. There was sometimes a sexual aspect to the stories and situations, and Mike Hammer surely had an eye for the dames, but it never got all that hot.

I never read Mickey after high school. There was a gap there, nothing came out between 1952 and 1961. I did pick up one or two of the later books, but found them tedious, and not worth finishing.

With the early books, you finished them. You might or might not like them, might or might not admire the way they were written. But you finished them.

Q: *What do you get if you cross a Jehovah's Witness with an agnostic?*
A: *Someone who rings your doorbell for no apparent reason.*

It's hard not to equate the diminished impact of the later work with Mickey's emergence as a Jehovah's Witness. He was converted sometime in the 1950s by someone who did indeed come to his door, and remained devoutly committed to the faith throughout his life.

He always denied that the books changed as a result of his religion. And indeed Mike Hammer's code remains about the same, and the world of Spillane's fiction is still divided into good guys and bad guys, and the bad guys deserve what's coming to them, and damn well get it.

But something's different.

And why did those first books hit readers as hard as they did? We can talk about their energy, and how they had more drive than later Spillane, but lots of Mickey's contemporaries wrote tough books about driven, energetic characters. Many of them were superior stylists, too—for all that Ayn Rand, bless her heart, found a way to prove that Mickey was a better writer than Thomas Wolfe.

I keep coming back to a point I mentioned earlier, in my introduction to the Dutton omnibus. Spillane, whose first prose fiction was short-short stories for the comics, emerged as a novelist writing prose comic books for grown-ups. His readers had read comic books before they read novels, and they were predisposed to appreciate what he gave them. They responded full-out to the pace, the immediacy, even the lack of nuance.

Mickey was made a Grand Master of Mystery Writers of America in 1995.

Sixteen years later, it seems surprising that MWA waited so long. But that's not how it looked at the time. The notion of giving him this award was hugely controversial, and a substantial proportion of MWA's active membership regarded the whole notion as a travesty.

I was at a meeting, probably in the fall of 1994, probably at Bouchercon. If I remember correctly, it was an unofficial gathering of MWA people to consider the question. On one side, the pro-Spillane contingent argued that Mickey was enormously influential, that he had not only brought a whole generation of new readers to crime fiction but that in so doing he had spawned the whole world of hardboiled paperback original fiction. Gold Medal Originals, it was suggested, owed their very existence to the new market Mickey and Mike Hammer had called into existence.

I couldn't argue with that.

On the other side, the anti-Spillane crowd pointed out that, influential though they might well be, Mickey's books were essentially crap. The plots were dumb, the characters lacked any semblance of depth, the underlying philosophy was brutish, and the writing itself was heavy-handed and crude. Yes, the books were popular—or had been, decades ago. But it was not MWA's business to reward popularity. The marketplace did that. Our august organization gave out Edgars and designated Grand Masters in order to celebrate excellence, and these days it was hard to pick up a Mike Hammer novel and read it, let alone applaud its excellence.

I couldn't argue with that, either.

The debate, as I remember it, was surprisingly reasonable and well-mannered. The nays didn't shout too loud, because when all was said and done they liked Mickey, however little they thought of his work. And the yeas weren't that boisterous, either; while one or two might have concurred with Ayn Rand, most seemed to be arguing that Mickey should get the award irrespective of the quality of his work.

Well, come April he showed up at the annual dinner and was made a Grand Master. And all the anti-Spillane arguments were like snow in an Arctic summer; they didn't stop to melt, but sublimated, passing directly from a solid to a gaseous state. What, *not* give it to him? Who ever could have had an idea like that?

And I have to say he appreciated the honor. Well, why not? It came, after all, from the Mystery *Writers* of America.

If we'd been the Mystery *Authors* of America, it might have been a different story.

He was a hell of a nice guy. Did I mention that? It shouldn't go unsaid. One hell of a nice guy.

After the column ran in Mystery Scene, *I got an angry and bitter response from Mickey's widow, who felt I'd desecrated the corpse of a man who'd been a friend to me. I would not have written thus, she said, had Mickey still been alive.*

*I assume what riled her was my account of the ambiv-
alence preceding Mickey's Grand Master award—and it's
true, I would not have reported it if Mickey were around to
read it, for fear that he might find it hurtful.*

*When you're dead, you're past having your feelings hurt.
I was there in 1994, and the report's accurate.*

Ross Thomas

Ross died in 1995, two months before his 70th birthday. I found this first piece on my hard drive; it's clearly a eulogy I must have written at the time, but I have no idea where it may have appeared, though Mystery Scene's *a possibility. I did fly out to L.A. for his memorial service, but my remarks were extemporaneous.*

I first met Ross Thomas through his work. Sometime in the late '60s I picked up *Cast a Yellow Shadow,* the second novel about Padillo and McCorkle. I had somehow missed his stunning debut, *The Cold War Swap,* but I went out and fixed that at once. Not long afterward I got hold of a copy of the first of his books as Oliver Bleeck, *The Brass Go-Between.* On the jacket flap it said that Bleeck was a pseudonym. By the time I hit the third chapter I knew whose pseudonym it was. The Ross Thomas style was unmistakable.

Style's a hard thing to define. As the senator said of pornography, I may not be able to tell you what it is, but I know it when I see it. If pressed for a definition, I suppose I'd say that a writer's style is that stamp of his own personality borne by his writing.

Ross had style in abundance, and a splendid style it has always been. He never wrote a graceless sentence, never failed to present even the least significant of minor characters and bit players as a distinctive three-dimensional being. His stories are as tough-minded and cynical as anything on the dark side of noir, yet at the same time they positively sparkle with wit and humor.

We became acquainted in 1970 or '71. I sent him a book, and we discovered that each of us had been reading the other for a while. Nothing I know of bonds two writers as quickly as this mutual recognition. I saw Ross once or twice in Washington, and a couple of times in New York. I spent half a year in California after he and Rosalie had moved to Malibu, and I visited them there several times. In recent years we mostly encountered each other far from home—at Bouchercons and on book tours, and on foreign soil at conferences of the International Association of Crime Writers, in Spain and Cuba and the Yucatan.

In all, I don't suppose we met twenty times over twenty-five years, nor did we correspond or keep in touch by telephone. Yet I recognized Ross as a friend at our first meeting, and I always took delight every time we met, in person or in print.

His books, every single one of them, are of that small company of volumes one may read over and over and over, with no loss of pleasure in the repetition. I have them all and I will treasure them. But there won't be any more, and that saddens me. I miss the ones he didn't live to write, even as I will miss the dear sweet man himself.

Several years after Ross's death, Ruth Cavin at St. Martin's began reissuing his novels in handsome trade paperback editions, each with a foreword by an admiring writer. She was good enough to invite me to the party, and the novel I picked was Briarpatch. *It was published in 2003:*

Three or four times over the years, I got to hear Ross Thomas tell how he got started in the writing game. It was a pretty good story all by itself, but the best part about it for me was watching the faces of the wannabes in the audience.

Ross would explain that he'd been at loose ends after a job ended—maybe he'd just finished running a political campaign for a friend in Jamestown, North Dakota, or maybe he had recently returned from Africa—and he'd decided to try his hand at a novel. So he sat down and wrote one, and after a month or two he was done.

It occurred to him that it might be nice to have it published, but he wasn't sure how to proceed. So he called up a knowledgeable friend.

"I've written a book," he said, "and wondered what I ought to do next."

"Have a drink," the friend suggested. "Take an aspirin. Lie down, put your feet up."

"I thought I'd try to have it published," Ross told him.

"It has to be typewritten. And double-spaced."

It already was, Ross said. Whereupon, he told his listeners, the fellow told him how to proceed. He was to get some brown wrapping paper, wrap the manuscript neatly in it, and send it to a particular editor at a particular publishing house.

So he did.

And, two weeks later, there was a letter in his mailbox, from the editor to whom he'd sent the manuscript in its plain brown wrapper. "He said they would like to publish my novel," Ross reported, "and that they would be sending a contract."

No wannabe wants to hear a story like that. If you want to win the hearts and minds of struggling writers, you're better advised to tell them of your own struggles—the failures and false starts, the endless parade of rejections, the paralyzing bouts with writer's block and alcoholism and the heartbreak of psoriasis. Finally, against long odds, after enduring and somehow surviving more perils than Pauline and more tsuris than Job, finally the writer prevails, the book is published, and can't you hear the violins?

Well, tough. Ross told it as it happened, and he could have been a lot harder on them. He could have gone on to say that the manuscript in question was published as *The Cold War Swap*, that it was widely praised and won the Edgar Allan Poe award as best first novel of the year, and that it launched a career that brought him no end of awards, an army of fiercely loyal readers, and a whole shelf of books with his name on them, in none of which one will ever encounter an ill-chosen word, an infelicitous phrase, or a clunky sentence.

Because Ross was far too modest to say any of that, some of those wannabes shook their heads and told themselves how lucky he'd been. Yeah, right. The way Ted Williams was lucky at baseball, or Nijinsky at ballet. Lucky bastards, the lot of them.

When Ross died, many years sooner than anyone would have wished, one of the things we told each other at his memorial service was that, while we wouldn't have the presence of this dear friend, wouldn't have a new book to look forward to each year, we'd still have the books he'd written.

I suppose we always say that when a writer dies, and, while it's as inarguable as that Bogie and Bergman will always have Paris, it's generally about as much comfort. Because most books, however enjoyable and compulsively readable as they are first time around, don't offer that much when reread.

But there are exceptions. I'm not sure what it is that makes a writer rereadable, but I do know that I especially cherish those writers whose books I can read with pleasure over and over and over. There aren't many of them, and I'm grateful for every one.

Ross Thomas is high on that short list. I've read some of his books three and four times, and expect to read them again.

Briarpatch, as it happens, was one I'd read only once. It was published in 1984, and I bought it as soon as it came out, and must have read it as soon as I had an uninterrupted evening. My library has been purged several times since then, in the course of several relocations, but I always kept all of Ross's books, so my copy was on the shelf when Ruth Cavin invited me to write an introduction for it. (The opportunity to read it again was not the least of my reasons for agreeing.)

And, wonder of wonders, I did not remember one single word of it!

While I'm not entirely thrilled with what this may imply about my ongoing mental capacity, it meant I had the great pleasure of reading a new Ross Thomas novel. And it was a pleasure indeed, and one I should cease to detain you from having for yourself. I don't know if I have more treats of this nature in store for me—a quick glance at my Ross Thomas shelf would seem to suggest that I have retained at least a little of all the others, but who's to say what a few more years of senescence might not accomplish for me?

Enough! I invite you to enjoy *Briarpatch*, whether for the first or the tenth time. It's a wonderful book by a man who wrote no other sort.

And, when I began writing my column for Mystery Scene, *I picked Ross for the second entry:*

Remembering Ross Thomas

Ross Thomas didn't do a lot of public speaking, and maybe it's just as well.

He was both good and bad at it—good in that he expressed himself well and spoke in paragraphs, not so good in that he didn't project, and was often hard to hear beyond the first few rows. But the worst thing about a Ross Thomas talk or interview was the number of people who'd walk out of it afterward yearning to kill themselves.

Writers, all of them. And what sent them home itching to swallow the Veronal was Ross's explanation of how he'd started out in the business. I heard him tell the story several times, and it generally came out something like this:

"I decided I'd like to write a book. I set up my typewriter and started hitting the keys, and when I was done I had a couple hundred double-spaced pages and didn't know what to do with them, so I called a writer friend of mine in New York and told him what I'd done. 'Now why would you do something like that?' he wondered. 'Well, go out and buy some brown wrapping paper, and wrap your manuscript in that. And then address the parcel to this fellow at William Morrow, in New York, and mail it to him. And enclose return postage, so he can send it back to you.'

"So I did that, making a reasonably neat parcel of it, and I sent it off, and a couple of weeks went by. Then I got a phone call from the chap I'd sent the manuscript to, and he said they wanted to publish my book."

Ah, the sweet agony of the literary life. The struggle, the disappointment, the never-ending cycle of hope and heartbreak.

Yeah, right.

So I sent it off, and this fellow called up and said they wanted to publish it. Many would sigh when they heard those words, and the loudest sighs came from those who knew what Ross was too modest to add, and what the late Paul Harvey would have called The End of the Story: The book was *The Cold War Swap,* and William Morrow did indeed publish it, and it went on to win the Edgar Allan Poe award for best first mystery of 1966.

Ross followed *The Cold War Swap* with *Cast a Yellow Shadow*, a second book about Padillo and McCorkle. It seems to me I read those two out of order, but after that I bought all his books as they came out. And one day in 1969 I came across a new book called *The Brass Go-Between*, by one Oliver Bleeck, identified by his publisher as the pseudonym of a well-known writer. The publisher was William Morrow, which would have constituted a clue, but it was a clue I doubt I'd have needed. I opened the book, read two or three pages, knew at once just what well-known writer had written these words, and bought the book and took it home.

I was a fan, and a year or two later I wrote a fan letter. I learned from someone at Morrow that Ross was living in London, got his address, and sent him the letter, along with a copy of my new book. I got a response that made it clear that he had been enjoying my work over the years, and that sort of mutual admiration is not the worst foundation for a friendship.

A couple more letters crossed the Atlantic, and my then-wife and I enlarged a planned trip to Ireland to include a couple of days in London. Ross had a flat in Kensington, if I remember correctly, and was sharing it with a woman and a couple of cats. I think the woman's name was Judy. Or maybe that was one of the cats.

Well, it was close to forty years ago, and I was drinking back then. But Ross, to my considerable surprise, was not. He poured drinks with a generous hand, made sure my glass was never empty (even as I made sure it didn't remain full for long), and treated us to an elegant dinner at Prunier's, where he consulted with the sommelier and chose the wine.

But he didn't have any wine himself, or any whisky, or even a glass of light ale. Nothing stronger than a postprandial espresso.

Now I knew some people who didn't drink. I found their behavior curious, but I figured they had their reasons. One fellow I knew got drunk once, didn't like it, and decided never to do it again. I could understand that, even if I had a little trouble imagining what it was he didn't like about it.

But the novels I'd read, whether by Ross Thomas or Oliver Bleeck, displayed throughout a deep familiarity and abiding affection for ethyl alcohol in all its forms. Ross's characters drank, and drank a lot, and did so pretty much all the time.

I didn't get it. The man was no Mormon; he drank a lot of coffee and smoked one Pall Mall after another, but he didn't drink.

Did I ask him about it? It seems to me I probed just enough to learn that he didn't drink these days. I wondered why, but felt it would be unseemly to ask.

The next time I saw Ross was a year or so later. I was on a weekend visit to Washington with my daughter Amy, staying at the Hay-Adams across the street from the White House. (I didn't have any money, but hotels were cheap, and it seems to me our room at the Hay set me back all of $35 a night. Nowadays it would be twenty times that, and I couldn't possibly afford it.) We spent an evening together, and I had a couple of drinks, and he didn't, but I no longer found it remarkable. I had grown used to the idea. Some people didn't drink, and he was evidently one of them, although his characters were very convincing drinkers. Well, what of it? Edgar Rice

Burroughs had never been to Africa—or, come to think of it, to Mars, either. You didn't have to go there to write about it, did you?

In the late '60s I bought a farmhouse on 20+ acres near Lambertville, New Jersey, and Ross and Judy were going to visit, but I can't remember whether they did or not. There are, alas, some burnt-out bulbs in the streetlights on Memory Lane. But in 1973 my marriage ended and I moved to West 58th Street, and by then Judy was no longer part of the equation, and one day the following year I got a phone call from Ross, demanding to know what was the finest restaurant in New York.

I wasn't the best person to ask, but I told him Lutece was probably the best, or close to it.

"Make a reservation," he announced, "for tomorrow at one. I'll be taking you and your girl to lunch."

The woman I was seeing had a job she couldn't abandon, but I knew a recent divorcée, a big Ross Thomas fan, who would certainly be up for a meal. I made the reservation, and Ross said he'd pick me up at my apartment around noon.

He came by around eleven-thirty. He rang my doorbell and I opened the door and there was Ross, with his eyes rolling around in his head. "We've got nothing to worry about," he announced. "I just laid twenty bucks on your doorman."

And just like that I understood why he didn't drink.

The details of the afternoon are a little vague, and I can't blame that on the years, because they were vague from the jump. Ross was accompanied by a young man he called the Sergeant-Major, for indiscernible reasons, who seemed to be a sort of driver and bodyguard. The Sergeant-Major went off to do something, and Ross had a seat, and I drank everything I could find in an effort to catch up, because I felt entirely too sober for the company. There was nothing on hand but a few cordials I kept for company, half-pint bottles of Kirschwasser and Goldwasser and Triple Sec, the sort of thing of which nobody would want more than a sip or two, but I braced myself and Made Do.

The Sergeant-Major turned up in time to drive us to Lutece in a limo, picking up my friend Debby en route, where he left us to do something else. (He was armed, Ross told us, and got his gun through airport security—such as it was in those innocent days—by wearing it in an ankle holster.)

At Lutece, they seated the three of us at a lovely table upstairs, and a waiter came to take our drink order. Ross said he wanted a triple vodka martini, straight up and extra dry. The waiter asked if he'd prefer an olive or an onion with that. "We'll eat later," Ross announced.

And after that, alas, it all gets rather vague. Ross was in the middle of a two- or three-week toot, and I was no match for him. I blotted my copybook, falling asleep with my head in a plate of Chicken Kiev, but not until I'd had one or two bites of it. It was a specialty at Lutece, and rightly so.

Mencken wrote somewhere that the hand of the Lord had taken hold of the United States by the state of Maine, and lifted, so that everything loose wound up in Southern California. I was loose enough to qualify, and two years after that lunch I was living in Hollywood at the Magic Hotel, and my three daughters came out to spend the summer with me. We spent July at the hotel and August driving back across the country to New York, and it was in July that we went out to Malibu for the day.

Ross was living there with Rosalie, who'd been with the Library of Congress in Washington, and who had since become Mrs. Thomas. They had rented a beachfront cottage in a community called Pirate Cove—it's right there in the opening scene in *Chinaman's Chance,* so there's no need for me to describe it. I had driven out myself for a visit sometime in May or June, but I remember the July trip more vividly. My girls were 15, 13, and 6 at the time, and I guess they were at their most charming, because over the years Ross and

Rosalie never ceased asking about them, and remembering what a grand day we'd all spent together.

In Malibu, Ross mentioned the lunch at Lutece, and confided that his spree had been physically and financially ruinous. But, he said a little wistfully, it was fun while it lasted.

As far as I know he never drank again. I drove the girls back to New York in August, and wound up moving back to Manhattan, and in the spring of '77 I stopped drinking. The only person I could think to tell was Ross, and I wrote him a letter and got an immediate reply. "I went for the cookies and the coffee," he said of the group he'd joined, "but what I really like are the stories, where a guy tells how he was down and out in East St. Louis, and now he's president of IBM with rising expectations."

As a writer, Ross was elegantly perverse. He wrote wonderfully tough-minded and uncompromisingly realistic fiction and peopled it with characters with names every bit as unlikely as Nicely-Nicely Johnson and Pussy Galore. I suppose it's possible to have a police chief named Homer Necessary, but the fellow turns up in the same book as Lucifer Dye. (The book is *The Fools in Town Are on Our Side,* and it's my favorite of them all; a spin on Hammett's *Red Harvest,* it boasts a backstory that's a fine novel all by itself.)

Ross insisted that he picked colorful names so that he'd remember them while he was writing. But I think he just liked them.

Early on, he reported, some old editor took him aside and gave him a piece of advice. "Two things you never want to write about," said the fellow, who may well have had something to drink before imparting this bit of wisdom. "Dwarves and Chinamen. Nobody wants to read about dwarves or Chinamen."

Ross thanked the fellow and assured him he'd never forget it. And the next novel he wrote was *The Eighth Dwarf,* and he followed it with *Chinaman's Chance.*

*   *   *

In one of the Oliver Bleeck books, two wonderfully engaging friends of the protagonist turn up and join him in a rescue operation in Yugoslavia. The banter among the three is a delight, and the reader looks forward to more of it in later books—until, after the plot has been successfully resolved, a stray bullet zips in and kills one of the buddies.

Why???

"I could just picture these clowns joking around in book after book," he told me, "and I decided the hell with all that, so I nipped it in the bud."

Ross's life before *Cold War Swap* informed his work; he'd been to Africa and Singapore and Germany, and knew most of the places he wrote about. Rumors abounded that he'd been with the CIA, and I gather his response if asked was an enigmatic smile, but I never asked and in fact rarely gave it much thought. I'm sure his work in Africa put him in contact with some of the Langley crowd, for whom he had a contempt that could only have been born of familiarity. But I'd be surprised if he had any real connection with the Company.

But of course one never knows.

I wish I'd seen more of him over the years, but we were on opposite coasts, so our contacts were infrequent. I ran into Ross now and then at Bouchercon, and when a book tour took him to New York or me to L.A.—or, on one occasion, put us both in D.C. at the same time. Ross was a founding member of the International Association of Crime Writers, and Lynne and I spent time with him and Rosalie on IACW excursions to Spain and Cuba.

In 1985, eighteen years after his first Edgar, Ross won again for best novel with *Briarpatch*. In his acceptance speech he said he was grateful MWA felt his work hadn't deteriorated over the years.

And it never did. He was always at the top of his game, and never wrote a bad sentence or a lifeless page, never created an unengaging character. He died in December of 1995. Too soon, I'd say—but that's how it is with the people one likes and admires.

The books live on. That's what we always say, isn't it? But in Ross's case it's true. They're endlessly rereadable, every one of them. Especially—no, I'm not going to pick a favorite. They're all wonderful.

Jim Thompson

In my 1993 American Heritage piece, "My Life in Crime,"
I included Jim Thompson in my list of favorite American
crime writers, with the caveat that he'd made the very
American leap from neglect to unquestioning adoration.
I'd said so in more detail in a 1990 piece for the New York
Times Book Review:

In *Bad Boy*, a memoir of his early years, the crime-fiction writer Jim Thompson tells of a West Texas deputy sheriff who pursued him when, as a young man, he neglected to pay a fine for getting drunk and disturbing the peace. Alone with him on the vast prairie, the deputy becomes a creature of menace:

" 'Lived here all my life . . . . Everyone knows me. No one knows you. And we're all alone. What do you make o' that, a smart fella like you? . . . What do you think an ol' stupid country boy might do in a case like this?' "

The deputy grins, puts on a pair of gloves, smacks a fist into the palm of his other hand.

" 'I'll tell you something . . . . Tell you a couple of things. There ain't no way of telling what a man is by looking at him. There ain't no way of knowing what he'll do if he has the chance. You think maybe you can remember that?' "

Later, Thompson tries to figure out what has happened. Was the deputy trying to throw a scare into him? Or did the scene the two played come very close to murder?

> "The riddle, of course, lay not so much in him as me. I tended to see things in black and white, with no intermediate shadings. I was too prone to categorize—naturally, using myself as the norm. The deputy had behaved first one way, then another, then the first again. And in my ignorance I saw this as complexity instead of simplicity.
>
> "He had gone as far as his background and breeding would allow to be amiable. I hadn't responded to it, so he had taken another tack. It was simple once I saw things through his eyes instead of my own.
>
> "I didn't know whether he would have killed me, because he didn't know himself."

Thompson tried to write about the man in his early novels, but couldn't get him right. Thirty years later, that West Texas lawman would emerge as his single most memorable character, Lou Ford, the psychopathic deputy sheriff in *The Killer Inside Me* (1952).

Jim Thompson is a hot ticket these days. Several of his books have recently been filmed. Others are before the cameras now, and most of the rest have been optioned. Two biographies of the author are scheduled for publication. Many of his books are back in print. Others will be reissued soon.

Born in Oklahoma in 1906, Thompson began writing in his teens but did not publish his first novel until he was 36. Of his 29 books, more than half were published in the 1950s, and a total of 10 books saw print in 1953–54 alone. His third novel, *Nothing More Than Murder,* was published by Harper in 1949, and the Dell reprint carries a blurb from the *Book-of-the-Month Club News*. All his other books, however, were paperback originals, many published by Lion Books. They were rarely reviewed, brought the author very little money, and had the shelf life of pulp magazine fiction.

In his later years Thompson wrote only a handful of books, and several of those were novelizations of films and television shows. He was 70 when he died 14 years ago; all his books were out of print.

If he was gone, he was not entirely forgotten. Thompson had made a strong impression on some readers, not a few of them crime writers themselves. The cult of fans grew substantially when Black Lizard Books (a small Chicago press now part of Vintage Books) reprinted several of his strongest books in the mid-1980s. Suddenly, he seems to be everybody's favorite writer, and the actor Sean Penn has raved that *"The Killer Inside Me"* is "the best book I've ever read." What's all the fuss about? Not brilliant writing. Thompson wrote very quickly, and his works show the faults as well as the virtues of fast writing. He often provides a strong driving narrative and crisp dialogue, but frequently mars the effect with patches of awful writing, slapdash characterization and clumsy plotting.

The writing aside, Thompson at his best casts the coldest possible eye on life and death and offers us an unsparing view of the human condition. The titles alone are hardboiled evocations of their genre and their time: *Savage Night, A Hell of a Woman, After Dark, My Sweet, A Swell-Looking Babe.* When his characters are not pure psychopaths, they still tend to be criminals, caught up in forces beyond their control and their understanding, killing not so much out of passion or avarice, but because it seems like a good idea at the time or because circumstances afford them no choice.

In *Pop. 1280* (1964), the menacing deputy of Thompson's youth returns in the person of Nick Corey, another homicidal sheriff. When another character asks whether the force of circumstances can excuse immoral actions, Nick replies:

> " 'Well . . . do you excuse a post for fittin' a hole? Maybe there's a nest of rabbits down in that hole, and the post will crush 'em. But is that the post's fault, for fillin' a gap it was made to fit?'
>
> " 'But that's not a fair analogy, Nick. You're talking about inanimate objects.'
>
> " 'Yeah?' I said. 'So ain't we all relatively inanimate, George?

Just how much free will does any of us exercise? We got con-
trols all along the line, our physical make-up, our mental make-
up, our backgrounds; they're all shapin' us a certain way, fixin'
us up for a certain role in life, and George, we better play that
role or fill that hole or any goddang way you want to put it or all
hell is going to tumble out of the heavens and fall right down on
top of us. We better do what we were made to do, or we'll find
it being done to us.' "

And later:

"There were the helpless little girls, cryin' when their own
daddies crawled into bed with 'em. There were the men beating their wives, the women screamin' for mercy. There were the
kids wettin' in the beds from fear and nervousness, and their
mothers dosin' 'em with red pepper for punishment. There
were the haggard faces, drained white from hookworm and
blotched with scurvy . . . . I shuddered, thinking how wonderful
was our Creator to create such downright hideous things in the
world, so that something like murder didn't seem at all bad by
comparison."

Nick Corey, killing almost dispassionately, thinks he is doing
God's work. An unprejudiced sort, he champions a black man who is
being bullied; later he kills the bully, and when the black man turns
out to have witnessed the act, kills him too with no regret. By the
book's end he sees himself as Christ returned to earth, shepherding
souls to judgment.

Thompson's characters are holdup men and small-time grifters,
corrupt lawmen, punch-drunk fighters, escaped lunatics. They lead
horrible lives, do awful things and come to bad ends. Typically, there
are no winners in a Thompson novel. Even the innocent are guilty,
and no one gets out alive.

In *The Nothing Man* (1954), the narrator is a reporter, emas-
culated in the war and permanently embittered. In the course of
the book he thinks he has murdered three people, only to find out
at the end that he hasn't killed anyone; one was killed by another

character, one committed suicide, one died accidentally. Even in acts of violence, he proves impotent.

In *The Getaway,* bank robbers turn on one another as a matter of course. Two survive, a husband and wife who reach sanctuary in Mexico. But the place turns out to be hell; they can't leave, and the need to betray each other in order to stay alive destroys their love.

Perhaps we're more ready to listen to Thompson's message than we were 30 years ago. Perhaps his vision, relentlessly bleak, fits our times better than his own. Or maybe any generation is more willing to accept such a message from a distance.

For my own part, I liked Thompson better before the world decided he was a genius. His books pack more of a punch if you pick them up for two bits and come to them with no expectations. Today, though, his quirky little paperbacks can't measure up to the hype. When a cover blurb calls him "the best suspense writer going, bar none," the impulse to strike a revisionist pose is almost overwhelming.

But to hell with that. Jim Thompson, who received too little recognition during his lifetime, is getting rather too much of it now. So what? He still has things to tell us; his books are worth reading. Just keep in mind that it ain't Shakespeare.

Donald E. Westlake

Don Westlake and I were close friends for fifty years, from the day we introduced ourselves in the anteroom of Scott Meredith's office. We bonded instantly and the bond deepened with time. There was a stretch of a couple of years in the late '60s when we didn't speak, and some people claim there was a woman to blame, but we got over it.

Then he died during a family vacation in Mexico on the last day of 2008, and the following afternoon I got a phone call from Otto Penzler. Later that day—or perhaps it was the following day—Margery Flax at MWA requested an obit for their newsletter.

Here's what I wrote:

When the phone call came and brought the bad news, one of the first things that came to mind was John O'Hara's line: "George Gershwin died yesterday, but I don't have to believe that if I don't want to."

I certainly don't want to believe my old friend Don is gone. He's been a part of my life for fifty years. We met in the waiting room at the Scott Meredith agency; we had both worked there, though not at the same time, and we'd both managed the transition from employee to client, and now we introduced ourselves and walked out of there and into a friendship. By then we had already sold our first appalling books to the same venal publisher, and seen our first weary stories appear in the same dreary magazines. We had a lot to talk about, and that never changed.

What a wonderful writer he was. He fell into crime fiction, that's how most of us got there back in the day, but I swear I think he could have written anything. In 1963, he sent me the manuscript of a novel he'd just completed. The title was *Memory*, and it was a dark and gripping novel about a man suffering from amnesia. He was at once attempting to build a new life for himself and find out who he was and where he'd come from, and it was a fool's errand indeed, because he kept losing memories of his new life as he went along.

I don't remember the details, I read it just once, and 45 years ago, but (barring that build-up of amyloid plaques that haunts us all) I'll never forget the book's impact. It was a powerful existentialist novel, let me tell you, and the reason you haven't read it—the reason nobody's teaching it right now in college courses—is that it never got published. Here was a long dark novel by a young writer no one had ever heard of, represented by an agent with little clout in the world of serious literature.

Years later Don's agent told him the world had changed, and he could now probably find a publisher for *Memory*. And Don read it over and decided it was a creature of its time, and that its time had come and gone. I never agreed with the decision, but it was his to make, and he made it.

Maybe someone will dig it out and publish it now. I don't think he'd mind. And I'd like the chance to read it again.

I suspect his career would have been different if *Memory* had been published back when it was written. Some years later Don wrote three or four stories about young people in relationships, and they made the rounds of the magazines, and they all came back. So he stopped—not because he didn't want to write the stories, but because he didn't get any more ideas. If *Memory* had succeeded, his unconscious would have supplied him with more ideas in a similar vein. When it didn't, other things came to him instead.

And here's the thing: He sat down to write every day, and for over half a century he never wrote a clumsy sentence or a dull paragraph or a tedious book. It is surely not the only test of a book's merits that you can read it with enjoyment more than once, but it is a very real test, and Don's books always aced it. Every couple of years I read the whole Parker series all the way through, and I suspect I'll go on doing this.

And how I'll miss the man who wrote them. He was a very dear friend. His company, off the page as well as on it, was always engaging, always a delight.

Seventy years have passed since O'Hara wrote those words about Gershwin, elevating denial to the level of a public virtue. O'Hara has been gone himself since 1970. Yet the line endures—and so do *Porgy & Bess* and *Rhapsody in Blue*, and *Appointment in Samarra* and *From the Terrace*. And so will the Parker books and the Dortmunder books, and *The Ax* and *Dancing Aztecs* and *Adios, Scheherezade* and *Baby, Would I Lie?* and . . . oh, you get the idea. Make your own list.

Donald Westlake died New Year's Eve, and I have to believe it, whether I want to or not. But I don't have to like it.

I don't know what triggered a memory of Memory, *but I'm glad it came to mind, glad I wrote about it. Abby Westlake, who'd never heard tell of the novel, read what I'd written and went to Don's files. The man kept everything, and his files were always in perfect order, and damned if she didn't find a raggedy-ass carbon of* Memory. *I looked at it, and there it was, the book I remembered. I showed it to Charles Ardai, and in due course Hard Case Crime published the book, and I commend it to your attention.*

While awaiting its publication, I wrote about Donald and Memory *for* Mystery Scene:

Remembering *Memory*

It was sometime in the spring of 1963 that the mailman brought me the carbon copy of a 300-plus page manuscript. He brought it to

48 Ebling Avenue, in Tonawanda, New York, where I'd been living with my wife and daughter for a little more than a year. My wife was pregnant—our second daughter would be born on Memorial Day. I was writing a lot and doing reasonably well with it, producing erotic fiction for a couple of publishers, short stories for crime fiction magazines, and the occasional book of fabricated sexual case histories under a medical pen name. The house was a good one on an attractive lot, and while the marriage may have been doomed, I didn't yet realize it. All I lacked was the companionship of other writers. I'd had that in New York, and had thrived on it, and back in Buffalo I felt the deprivation.

The manuscript that turned up in my mailbox was from my closest friend, Donald Westlake. Before the move to Tonawanda, Don and I had lived a very long subway ride apart, he and his wife and two sons in Canarsie, half a mile from the last stop on the Fourteenth Street line, my wife and daughter and I at 444 Central Park West, which at the time was a luxurious building in a neighborhood that wasn't quite good enough to be called marginal. By the time we moved, the Westlakes were preparing a move of their own, to a house in Englishtown, New Jersey. A fair amount of mail went back and forth between Tonawanda and Englishtown, but it wasn't the same.

Now the day Don sent me a copy of the book he'd just finished, for that's what the manuscript was, had been a day like any other day, with the exception that I'd been having chest pains. I was not yet 25 years old, and an unlikely candidate for a heart attack, but I had this occasional unpleasant sensation on the left side of my chest, and I managed to worry about it, and indeed called my doctor and arranged to come over the following day. (And let me spare you any unwarranted suspense. There was nothing wrong with me, and decades were to pass before it finally dawned on me that those symptoms, and other intimations of mortality around that time, almost certainly derived from the sudden and wholly unexpected death of my father a little over two years earlier.)

Here's the point: Don's manuscript arrived, and we had dinner and put the kid to bed, and I started reading. And my wife went to bed, and I stayed up reading, and after a while I forgot I was having a heart attack, and just kept reading until I finished the book around dawn. And somewhere along the way I became aware that my friend Don, who'd written a couple of mysteries and some science fiction and his fair share of soft-core erotica, had just produced a great novel.

And then, of course, nothing happened.

I don't know what Don expected. I myself assumed someone would publish the book, and that it would get good strong reviews, and be generally well received. I don't think I expected *Memory* would make Don rich, but then this was almost fifty years ago, and I don't think any of our crowd saw writing as a road to wealth. A year or so earlier, I was in Don's upper flat in Canarsie when he confided that he felt he'd arrived as a writer, that his future was secure. "I think," he said tentatively, almost reluctant to speak the words aloud, "that if I just keep on with what I've been doing, I can be fairly sure of bringing home ten grand a year."

What I never foresaw—and I doubt Don did, either—was that his agent would be unable to find a publisher for *Memory*.

But that's what happened, and in retrospect it's not all that hard to understand why. Henry Morrison, who represented Don at the time, was younger than his client, and his experience as an agent was largely with genre fiction. More to the point, Henry worked for Scott Meredith, who ranked in the more elevated literary circles a few rungs lower than pond scum.

Henry tried hard, and sent the manuscript all over the place, and most of the editors who read it thought it was terrific. Many of their responses contained the words "I wish I could publish this" in one form or another. But that sort of expression of regret was as far as their enthusiasm could carry them. They all sent *Memory* back where it came from.

Because what it was, when all was said and done, was a rather lengthy novel with no marketable topical hook by an author whose track record was substantially less than useless. (Don had published several hardcover mysteries with Random House, a top publisher, but this was no recommendation in the world of Serious Literature, not in 1963. One of the books, *The Mercenaries* (now available from Hard Case Crime under Don's original title, *The Cutie*), had been shortlisted for the Edgar for best first novel. Impressive? Now, perhaps, but less so a half century ago. Back then, the Edgar award was something about which nobody outside of MWA gave the northern end of a southbound rat. But for the small group of people who wrote them and the somewhat larger group of folks who read them, mysteries got about as much respect as Rodney Dangerfield.

On the other hand, publishing was less corporate back in the day, and a publisher could take a chance, and even bring out a book he knew he'd lose money on just because he thought it ought to be out there where people could read it. So I still find it curious that nobody would buy the book. Why didn't Random House publish it, if just to keep the author happy and add a little literary-world luster to his mystery-world reputation?

Never mind. The manuscript kept coming back, like a bad penny, or swallows to Capistrano. And eventually Henry ran out of places to send it.

Years later—late 1970s, it must have been—Henry told Don that he thought he could probably find a publisher for *Memory*. He had long since parted company with Scott Meredith, and Don's stature in the mystery field had grown considerably. And the mystery itself was rather less of a red-haired stepchild in the world of letters.

Don told me this, and told me too that he'd had a look at the book and decided its time had come and gone, that it was too dated in too many respects to be published.

I wasn't sure that was so. It seemed to me that the novel's virtues were enduring ones. But I hadn't read it since 1963, so what did I know?

(I should probably add, right about now, that Henry has not the slightest recollection of any of this. He doesn't remember the novel, nor does he recall that there was ever a book of Don's he'd been unable to sell, let alone that he wanted to try again fifteen years down the line. "This was a book I couldn't sell?" he said. "Well, why on earth would I remember something like that?" Memory indeed!)

Don died suddenly on the last day of 2008. Within days someone at MWA asked me to write something about him for *The Third Degree*. In the piece I talked about Don's great versatility as a writer, and how his career might have taken different turns but for certain bumps in the road. In that context I told about *Memory*, and what Don might have written if its reception had been less discouraging.

I emailed a copy to Don's widow, Abby, and told her someone might read it and make an effort to locate *Memory*, so she should prepare herself for inquiries in that regard. None came, as it happened, but this was the first Abby had heard of the book, and when she came upon a carbon copy of the manuscript in Don's considerable files, she knew what it was. Would I like to read it?

It was, I must say, a bedraggled copy. I don't suppose there are many of us left who actually remember carbon paper, and I have to tell you I don't miss it a bit. It was indispensable for years, and every time I came to the end of a page, I slipped a sheet of it between a sheet of good typing bond and a sheet of cheap manila paper—second sheets, we called the cheap stuff—and inserted the ensuing sandwich into the typewriter. It was many years before low-cost photocopying would allow me to dispense with carbon paper, and just a few more years before I could get rid of the typewriter, too. And now, with electronic submission, one barely needs paper, and with ebooks one won't need anything printed, and—

Never mind.

It was bedraggled, and some of the pages were torn and scotch-taped, and others were torn and untaped. And Don, like most of us, sometimes tried to get too many copies out of a sheet of carbon paper, so some of the pages were harder to read than others. But, by God, it was the book, and it was all there, and it was legible enough for me to recognize it as the book I'd read forty-five years earlier, and it was still the great novel I remembered.

Now what?

The first thing I realized was that the manuscript would have to be scanned. It was very hard to read in its present state, and the pages were in any case too fragile to survive many readings. Photocopying would just create an even less legible copy. Scanning seemed the answer, and I tried to do just that, but either my scanner or my competence therewith proved unequal to the task.

So I thought of Charles Ardai. I knew him to be a great fan of Don's, knew he'd been delighted to republish some of Don's early titles at Hard Case, and saw him as the ideal publisher for *Memory*.

And it didn't seem to me to be too much of a stretch for Hard Case. While *Memory* fits Otto Penzler's definition of a mystery, in that a crime or the threat of a crime is an important element of its plot, it is far more an existential novel than a work of category fiction. The plot, I should tell you, concerns an actor in a road company who is surprised in *flagrante delicto* by a jealous husband, and who barely survives a vicious beating that leaves him with a devastating and ongoing case of amnesia. It is the hero's desperate and doomed attempt to get his life back that is the story of *Memory*.

A mystery? Perhaps not, but nevertheless a book that is quintessentially noir. And it not only takes place in the 1960s, but was written then—as were so many of the books Hard Case publishes so effectively. So, with Abby Westlake's permission, I got in touch with Charles. At the very least, I figured I could euchre him into getting the book scanned.

Charles loved the book, felt it was important it be published, and agreed that it could find a home in his list. The advance reviews have been outstanding, and that's as much as I feel I need to say about the book, because you can go out and read it yourself. And I hope you do.

And still, you know, it leaves me wondering. About a couple of things.

First of all, I have to wonder how my old friend would feel about all this. You'll recall that there was a time when he told his agent not to seek a publisher for *Memory*, that it was hopelessly out of date, and that he'd rather let it remain unpublished. If it was dated twenty or more years ago, is it less dated now?

Arguably, it is. You could say that the extra time has worked to the book's advantage, that two more decades have transformed it from passé to period.

Still, it's his book, and he made his decision and never had occasion to countermand it. I think he'd be pleased to see the book vindicated, and made available to the reading public, but I'm just guessing. And the whole question's moot, isn't it? If there's an afterlife, I can't imagine it's one wherein the spirit spends a whole lot of energy caring what people are doing back on earth, and whether they're reading one's books.

(And *Memory's* publication is surely less likely to trouble Dan's ghost than another posthumous publishing project. Back in the day—way way back in the day—Don and I collaborated on a trio of soft-core erotic novels, writing alternate chapters and having great fun. Subterranean Press will be bringing out those books later this year in a triple volume, to be called *Hellcats & Honey Girls*. Would Don be happy about that? Sheesh, I'm not even sure I'm happy about it.)

What else do I wonder? Well, I once again find myself wondering what would have happened if *Memory* had been published at the time of its writing. I won't try to guess what its reception might have been, whether it would have been in the running for a Pulitzer or a National Book Award, or would have had to be content with a small but respectable sale and positive but not earthshaking reviews. A *succès d'estime*, let us say.

How would it have changed Don as a writer?

It's tempting to say it would have had no effect, that a writer with Don's artistic integrity would write the books he'd been placed here to write, that success or failure along the way would not persuade him to write something that didn't appeal to him, or forego writing something that did. And that's largely true for many of us, at least on a conscious level.

But so much of the real work of writing gets done well below the level of consciousness. Success engenders success, and encouragement breeds ideas. I'm sure *Memory*, by being published, would have led to more dark existential masterpieces. I know this not only because that's pretty much how it works for everybody, but because one can see the pattern elsewhere in Don's career.

His enduring reputation, surely, is as a writer of comic mysteries. It's easy to lose sight of the fact that the first Donald E. Westlake novels were uncompromisingly hardboiled works, and that he published five of them (and five Parker books as well, as Richard Stark) before his first comic mystery, *The Fugitive Pigeon*.

Pigeon outsold his earlier books, and got more attention from reviewers. And the next book, *The Busy Body*, was another comic mystery, and it not only sold well but became the basis for a film. And, just like that, Don was a writer of comic mysteries. He still wrote hardboiled books, along with books that resist categorization, but *The Fugitive Pigeon* pointed his career in a direction it would never abandon.

Would he have written comic works no matter what? Well, probably. Like more than a few of us, he had both a light and a dark side, and could best fulfill himself by expressing both sides in his work. Still, the success of those early comic mysteries encouraged that source within to come up with funny ideas, and it never ceased to do so.

That's one example. Here's another, on the opposite side. In the mid-'60s, Don wrote three or four contemporary short stories. They didn't have a crime or mystery element, and in fact were stories about modern relationships. (I haven't read them in ages, and

suspect they've vanished from the earth, so I don't remember anything much about them, but they were about couples blundering
through romance, as I recall, and the characters were bright and
sympathetic, and the stories were fun.)

He wrote them not because he thought there was any particular
point in writing short stories. There wasn't, any more than there is
today. He wrote them because the ideas came along and engaged
him, and a short story takes days out of your life, not months, so why
not write them?

So he did, and nothing came of it. A couple of magazine editors
liked them, but not enough to buy them. And that was the end of
that.

"They were fun to write," Don told me at the time. "And I'd write
more, if I got an idea for another. But nobody bought the ones I'd
written, and whatever part of me was coming up with the ideas just
said the hell with it."

There's not much point, really, in trying to guess what Don might
have written under other circumstances. For my part, I'm happy
enough with what he did write—and happier still that *Memory* will
finally see the light of day.

*One of the happier publishing phenomena of recent years
has been the republication by University of Chicago Press of
the entire run of novels Don wrote as Richard Stark. There
were 28, 24 about a criminal named Parker, four about a
colleague of Parker's named Grofield. I was invited to write
a joint foreword to three of the books, but I found myself
with enough to say about the books and their author that
I wound up writing individual forewords for each of the
books:*

Butcher's Moon

One night around the end of 1960 or the beginning of 1961, I was
in a second-floor flat in Canarsie, an unglamorous part of Brooklyn,

located at the very end of the Canarsie Line, a part of the subway system which ran east across Fourteenth Street from Eighth Avenue, then crossed the river, and wound up running on elevated tracks all the way to Rockaway Parkway. (The train was subsequently designated the LL, until years later they took one of its letters away and it became the L. No one knows why, but I've always figured it was a cost-cutting move. Of such small economies are great savings made.)

I lived in Manhattan at the time, on Central Park West at 104th Street, so I had to take two subway trains and walk several blocks to get to that flat, but I did it often and without complaint because that's where Don Westlake lived. We'd been best friends since we met in our mutual agent's office in July of 1959, where we introduced ourselves before walking a few blocks to his flat in Hell's Kitchen. We sat around there and had a few beers and talked and talked and talked, and that was the pattern that prevailed over the months. I moved home to Buffalo, met somebody, got married. Don and his then-wife moved from an unsafe neighborhood to an inaccessible one. My then-wife and I set up housekeeping in New York, first on West 69th Street, then on Central Park West. And Don and I got together often, and had a few beers, and talked and talked and talked.

And that's what we were doing that night I was telling you about, out in Canarsie. We were young writers together—he was five years my senior, but had spent time in the Air Force—and we talked a lot about what we were doing, and sometimes showed our work to each other. "I started something new," Don said, and handed me ten or fifteen pages of typescript, featuring a fellow named Parker who's walking across the George Washington Bridge, into Manhattan. In the first sentence, a passing motorist offers Parker a lift, and Parker tells him to go to hell.

I thought the chapter was good, and said so, and asked its author if he knew where it was going.

"Sort of," he said. "I'll just keep writing and see where it goes."

Which is how we both worked, more often than not. Don called it the Narrative Push method, and it has a couple of virtues. For one, you can just sit down and start writing, as there's no need to work everything out in your mind ahead of time. And, as Theodore Sturgeon famously observed, if the writer doesn't know what's going to happen next, he needn't worry that the reader will know what's going to happen next.

"I like the character," Don said. "I don't think I'll have trouble finding things for him to do."

Indeed.

One thing Don found for Parker to do, at the book's end, was die.

And that would have made this the shortest series in the annals of crime fiction, but for an editor at Pocket Books with the splendid name of Bucklin Moon. Moon may or may not have been the first editor to read *The Hunter,* but he was certainly the first who wanted to buy it. But he had a request. Did Parker have to die? Could he get away at the end, and go on to star in a whole series of books? Two more at a minimum, say, because Moon was prepared to offer a three-book contract.

Don had already established that he liked Parker, and that he could find plenty of things for him to do. And he confided that he'd only killed Parker off at the book's end because he thought that's what you were supposed to do with that sort of antihero. So he agreed, and revised the ending, and wrote *The Man With the Getaway Face* and *The Outfit,* and Moon sat down and drew up another three-book contract. Parker, and Richard Stark, were off and running.

Ah, yes. Richard Stark.

The conventional wisdom these days is that Don created the Richard Stark pen name to distinguish the uncompromisingly hardboiled Parker novels from the bubbly frothy Westlakean comic mysteries.

Not exactly. The Parker series had six titles in print at Pocket Books by the time Random House published *The Fugitive Pigeon,* Don's first comedic effort. (Don's earlier Random House novels, starting with *The Mercenaries*, owe more to Hammett than to Wodehouse; they're about as light and bubbly as bathtub gin.)

And Richard Stark first saw print two or three years before *The Hunter*. His was no separate persona, no marketing ploy; on several occasions Don had more than one story slotted in a single issue of a magazine, and was asked to use a pen name on one of them. Thus Richard Stark.

I don't know if he originally intended to hang Richard Stark on *The Hunter*. He might have, simply because it was to be a paperback original and he'd been busy establishing his own name at Random House. But if Parker was to start in a multi-volume series, then of course he'd need a pen name.

As noted, off and running.

Let's flash forward a few years, shall we? To 1974, and *Butcher's Moon,* the book to which I am privileged to be writing an introduction, and of which you, Dear Reader, are fortunate to have a copy.

Fortunate, I should say, for a couple of reasons. For one, copies rank somewhere between hen's teeth and the Holy Grail in elusiveness. The book, published in hardcover by Random House, does not seem ever to have been reprinted. When copies come up for sale, the price is high.

More to the point, *Butcher's Moon* would be special even if it were not hard to come by. For over twenty years it looked to be the last book in the series, and while that would have been regrettable, at least Parker's saga would have ended on a high note. Because in addition to being, to my mind, the strongest book in a strong series, *Butcher's Moon* brings Parker's story to completion if not to an end. In its pages, the author manages to tell a gripping and satisfying story while at the same time summing up and resolving the fifteen Parker books that preceded it.

He does so by having Parker confront the book's central problem by bringing in characters from other books, subordinate criminals who've been his partners in other heists dating back to the early days of the series. (I read this book first as an Advance Reading Copy, and as I recall it was annotated; every time there was a reference to an earlier caper, a footnote referred the reader to the book in which the incident was described. I remember thinking that was a nice touch, but evidently someone somewhere along the line thought it was intrusive, and perhaps it was. In any event, the copy I own now is a first edition, and there aren't any footnotes.)

It is strong testimony to the quality of the Parker books that, even decades after encountering them, the supporting cast members remain so sharply etched in memory that one recalls them at once. It is often said in the theater that there are no small parts, only small actors, and one could easily adapt the remark to the field of prose fiction. There are no minor characters, only minor writers, and the extent to which Parker's cast members are always memorable and always wholly human demonstrates that there is nothing minor about them or their creator.

And that, if it's all the same to you, is all I'm going to say about *Butcher's Moon*. You've got the book in your hands, and I can't see why you'd want me to explain it to you. Westlake, in any of his work and under any of his names, is very nearly as accessible as Dr. Seuss. You don't need a study guide, or someone like me to point things out to you.

The one thing I can suggest to improve your experience of reading *Butcher's Moon* is that you set it aside and read the foregoing fifteen books first, in the order they were written. If you've never read them before, or if you missed a few titles along the way, you've got a treat in store for you; if you read them years ago and your memory's a bit tentative, you'll find them a treat a second time around. And it's easy to do this, as all of the earlier titles are back in print in handsome new trade paperback editions uniform with this one.

If you can't wait, well, go ahead and read *Butcher's Moon*. Why not? What the hell, you can always read it again.

Comeback

Back in 1991 I got a phone call from Kenneth Turan of the *Los Angeles Times Book Review*, wanting to know if I'd be interested in reviewing *Perchance to Dream*, Robert B. Parker's sequel to Raymond Chandler's *The Big Sleep*. I'd long been a great fan of both writers, but you might not have known that from my response. I said, "Review it? I don't even want to read it."

"I know what you mean," Kenny said.

"I don't think I could say anything good about it," I said, "and I don't want to say anything bad about anybody's work, which is why I've pretty much stopped doing reviews."

Well, he said, how about writing about something I already knew I liked? An appreciation of an old favorite, for a new feature they'd started? Could I think of something I'd like to praise in print?

I didn't have to think. "Don Westlake's Parker books," I said.

"Oh, perfect," Kenny said. "I love those books."

Me too.

I was on a book tour when we spoke, and when I got home I went to work on the assignment. It took me a long time. Not to write the piece, that was easy enough and the work of a couple of hours. But first I felt the need to refresh my memory—by sitting down with the complete sixteen-book series and reading them all in order.

Was this necessary? No, of course not. I could have written the article without opening a single one of the books, let alone reading all of them word for word. But the main reason I accepted the assignment was that it gave me excuse to revisit the books. That, really, was the payoff; the couple of bucks the paper paid me was sort of a bonus.

Writing the piece was pleasant enough, but rereading the books was a genuine treat. I knew going in that it wouldn't be disappointing, because I'd already read several of the books more than once. They were, as I'd already established to my satisfaction, eminently rereadable.

And what makes a book work a second time around? It helps, of course, if it's of excellent quality—but that in and of itself is no guarantee that it'll be enjoyable more than once. Suspense, whether of the nail-biting-edge-of-the-chair sort or the less urgent page-turning lure of What Happens Next, can wear thin once you've established that things do in fact work out, that the hero survives, that the bad guy gets what's coming to him, and that they all live happily ever after. The Parker books are as suspenseful as one could possibly want, but that's not enough to recommend them for repeat readings.

I think that it's similar to what makes series fiction work. Shakespeare, you'll recall, wrote *The Merry Wives of Windsor* because Queen Elizabeth wanted to see another play with Sir John Falstaff in it. She wanted to meet the character again, which is to say that she desired to repeat the happy experience she had with *Henry IV,* parts one and two—but in a sense by having that experience again for the first time.

We make our way through a series of books because we want to enjoy the company of a favorite character in a new situation. And we reread a book because we so enjoy that character and his world that they remain fresh to us. "Age cannot wither her, nor custom stale / Her infinite variety," said Enobarbus of Cleopatra, and so it is with the handful of fictional characters of whom we can read more than once.

I don't suppose anyone would mistake Parker for Cleopatra, or Falstaff either. But I sat down and read sixteen books in a row about him, all of which I'd read at least once before. And my enthusiasm for the enterprise never flagged.

It had, I must say, a bittersweet element to it. Because the Parker books, which began with *The Hunter* in 1962, had come to a halt a dozen years later with *Butcher's Moon.* There had been sixteen of them (along with four books of a spin-off series, about Alan Grofield), and seventeen years had already passed without a seventeenth.

As I remarked in my introduction to *Butcher's Moon,* that

volume was not a bad one with which to end a series; it brought back many of the subordinate characters from earlier books, and tied up enough loose ends to serve as a creditable finale. The only thing wrong with it was that the series was evidently over—and that was not at all what a reader would have preferred.

Nor, in point of fact, was it what the author himself would have preferred. While no evidence of this turned up in print, Don Westlake very much wanted to go on writing about Parker, and I know that he did indeed make a number of abortive attempts toward that end subsequent to *Butcher's Moon*. They all died on the vine after a couple of chapters. Now there are writers who might have finished those books, and might have dutifully turned out more books as long as someone was willing to publish them, but Westlake was not that sort of writer; he had to be engaged in a book in order to get it written. And that, I would submit, is very much a Good Thing. It is the writer's own engagement in his work that makes the work, well, engaging.

It wasn't until several years after my *LA Times* piece that Parker made his comeback in, duh, *Comeback*. During that hiatus of twenty-three years, Don continued to write books about John Dortmunder and his hapless gang; Dortmunder, who seemed at the time to have supplanted Parker, had come into existence in 1970, in an instance of the author's having made lemonade when fate—and Parker—handed him a lemon.

Here's what happened: Don was writing a novel in which Parker and his gang had to steal the same precious stone more than once. Things would go wrong, and they'd have to steal it again.

But there was a problem. It kept coming out funny, and if there was one thing a Parker book was not, funny was it. Downbeat, ironic, relentless, tough-minded—there were lots of adjectives that applied to Parker and his world, but funny was not among them.

So Don, who couldn't bear either to go on writing the book or to abandon it, did something quite brilliant. He rewrote the book with characters designed to fit a comic caper novel, called it *The Hot*

Rock, and was not displeased to see it published to great acclaim and snapped up for filming.

There were seven Dortmunder novels written and published during the twenty-three years of Parker's hibernation, or suspended animation, or what you will. And then one day Don had an idea for a Parker book, and started it, and found that it worked. He saw it through to completion, and the book was the one you are now holding in your hands. Parker had come back—and the title was almost inevitable.

What makes a series stop? And how does it return to life?

The subject is one I've had occasion to ponder, and not only as a disinterested observer. My own body of work includes several series. One of them, about an ex-cop named Matthew Scudder, runs to sixteen books. The fifth book, *Eight Million Ways to Die,* saw the hard-drinking protagonist confront his alcoholism and choose sobriety, and it seemed to me to bring the series to a close. I did manage a sixth book, a sort of prequel, but then there was a gap of several years before I suddenly found myself able to do what had seemed impossible, to write a seventh book and continue the series. Nine books later I again thought I was done, and again I proved myself wrong; a seventeenth Scudder novel, *A Drop of the Hard Stuff,* will be published in April of 2011.

The lacunae in Scudder's career are nothing compared to those in a couple of other series. Bernie Rhodenbarr, my lightfingered bookseller, spent eleven years on the shelf between *The Burglar Who Painted Like Mondrian* and *The Burglar Who Traded Ted Williams.* And between Evan Tanner's seventh appearance, *Me Tanner, You Jane,* and his return in *Tanner On Ice,* there yawned a gap of twenty-eight years.

Who knows why this happens, why a series stops, why it starts up again? It is, I submit, a mysterious process. Most of the choices a writer makes, and almost all of the important ones, are worked out on an unconscious level. The whole business of literary creation is sufficiently inexplicable that we might as well call it magic and let it go at that.

> "When the angel opened the door, Parker stepped first past the threshold into the darkness of the cinder block corridor beneath the stage . . ."

And just like that Parker's back, and we're right there with him. And I can tell you right now that he hasn't lost a step.

Backflash

In 1997, Donald Westlake published *Comeback,* his seventeenth novel about a professional thief named Parker. The title was remarkably apt, as twenty-three years had come and gone since *Butcher's Moon,* the sixteenth book in the series.

When Parker returned in *Comeback,* it was as if he'd never left. He was still very much himself, still happily coupled with Claire, still doing the same sort of work and leading the same kind of life between engagements. Nor was his return that of an old performer managing one last star turn before slipping into permanent retirement; on the contrary, he was back with a vengeance, and in the next decade seven more novels rolled out of their author's typewriter (a Smith-Corona manual portable, in case you were wondering) and took their place on bookstore shelves.

Backflash followed *Comeback* a year later, and was followed in turn by *Flashfire, Firebreak,* and *Breakout.* Does a subtle pattern begin to emerge? Don liked a certain amount of gimmickry in series titles, and the gimmick here was simple enough; each title would be a two-syllable compound word, with the second syllable of one book becoming the first syllable of the next. After *Breakout* in 2002, the next book would logically begin with *Out. Outcome* would have brought matters full circle, but I don't believe Don seriously considered it; instead he dropped the titular sequence and moved on to *Nobody Runs Forever.*

This was not the first title sequence for the series. The early books were all two-word titles, consisting of a noun preceded by *the*. *The Hunter, The Outfit, The Mourner, The Score, The Jugger, The Seventh, The Handle.* (And yes, I've omitted Book Two, *The Man With the Getaway Face.*) Then came a four-book Score sequence: *The Rare Coin Score, The Green Eagle Score, The Black Ice Score,* and *The Sour Lemon Score.* Then *Deadly Edge, Slayground, Plunder Squad,* and *Butcher's Moon.*

Title sequences serve chiefly to remind the reader that there's a series here, but they can serve other purposes as well. One of these is the author's personal amusement; it is by no means coincidental that *The Seventh,* so-called because the proceeds of a job are to be split seven ways, was indeed the seventh book of the series.

With the post-*Butcher's Moon* books, the linked titles helped keep the reader aware of the order of the books, with one title—and one book—leading to another. And, because in this particular instance Don thought of the next title before he knew what the book would be about, they helped lead him to his plot.

That's less obvious with *Backflash,* which suggests the word *flashback,* and in which the storyline doesn't particularly echo the title. Afterward, in *Flashfire* and *Firebreak,* the title and the plot are more closely linked, and *Breakout* is, obviously, about a breakout.

Nobody Runs Forever (2004) was an ominous title, suggesting that Parker's run might in fact be over. Not so. Two years later he was back in *Ask the Parrot,* and in 2008 he made his last appearance, in *Dirty Money.*

A few months later, on the last day of the year, Don died. Nobody writes forever.

> *When the car stopped rolling, Parker kicked out the windshield and crawled through onto the wrinkled hood, Glock first.*

Title patterns come and go over the two dozen Parker novels, but a couple of other elements have been more of a constant. The opening is one of these. In each book's initial sentence, something happens and Parker reacts. When this happened, Parker did this— and we're off and running.

> *When the guy with asthma finally came in from the fire escape, Parker rabbit-punched him and took his gun away.*
>
> *When the woman screamed, Parker awoke and rolled off the bed.*
>
> *When the bandages came off, Parker looked in the mirror at a stranger.*
>
> *When the knock came at the door, Parker was just turning to the obituary page.*
>
> *When the bellboy left, Parker went over to the house phone and made his call.*
>
> *When a fresh-faced guy in a Chevy offered him a lift, Parker told him to go to hell.*
>
> *When the helicopter swept northward and lifted out of sight over the top of the hill, Parker stepped away from the tree he'd waited beside and continued his climb.*
>
> *When the shit hit the fan, Parker threw himself in front of it.*

Well, no, I made up that last one. But you get the idea. When A, then B.

There are a few books that open differently—*The Black Ice Score, The Sour Lemon Score, Deadly Edge.* I don't think Don wanted to be a slave to anything, even if it were something of his own devising. A title sequence would be maintained until it became unwieldy, or tiresome; an opening would serve until a variation seemed to serve better.

If we can spot a pattern in openings and titles, so can we find one in the structure of the Parker books. Typically, they consist of four sections, and it is not much of a stretch to think of them as four movements of a symphony. The first two sections are told entirely from Parker's point of view, and in their course he settles on a criminal enterprise, assembles a crew, makes his plans and preparations, and have at it.

Then, in the third section (or sometimes the second), every episode is recounted from the point of view of one of the other characters. Parker may or may not be present in any of these scenes, but we're not privy to his thoughts and impressions. Instead, we watch the story unfold through the eyes of all the other players in the game, including both his partners and the players on the other side, as well as those citizens caught in the middle.

The fourth section returns us to Parker's point of view, as he does what he can to see things through to a favorable conclusion.

Not every book adheres strictly to this pattern—in *Deadly Edge,* for example, the non-Parker section is told entirely from the point of view of Claire, who is in jeopardy—but it's the template for most of the series. But for the word's unfortunate connotations, it would not be unfair to describe the books as formulaic.

To many readers, and not a few writers as well, the idea of a formula suggests that it makes things easy for the writer, that it reduces the need for imagination and creativity, that he who possesses a formula can simply dash off or grind out books as required, with no need to be inventive. The writer becomes a sort of blackjack dealer, hitting sixteen and staying with seventeen, scooping up losing bets and paying off winners, and, inevitably the beneficiary of a mathematical edge, coming out ahead in the end.

And, by God, anybody could do it, if only one possessed the formula. But, alas, it's as closely guarded as the formula for Coca-Cola.

Well, that's not how it works. First of all, one remarkable thing about prose fiction is that there are no secrets concealed in it. The process is wholly self-evident. You might wonder how a painter managed to achieve the particular luminescence on a particular canvas, but you can see at a glance how a writer achieved a given effect. He took these words—the ones you see on the page—and he put them in this particular order. And there you have it.

*   *   *

Parker doesn't age much in the course of the series. Time passes and his history accumulates, with characters recurring from book to book, but Parker remains pretty much the same unspecified age. Early middle age, I suppose. Forties, fifties. It doesn't much matter. He's always Parker.

Whether a series character will age or evolve is one of the decisions an author has to make. Among my own series, Bernie Rhodenbarr never gets a day older, while Matthew Scudder has aged in real time, going from his late thirties to his early seventies in the years I've been writing about him. (Sue Grafton found an interesting variant for Kinsey Millhone; Kinsey ages in real fictional time, but it takes three books for one year to pass; now, as the series nears its end, the books are set a couple of decades in the past.)

Parker's world changes, and that's how the early books show their age. There are no cell phones or credit cards, and it's a lot easier to live off the grid and fly under the radar. By the later books, it's hard to find anything to steal; big blocks of cash, there for the taking, are hard to come by in a credit economy.

Parker's world, it should be said, is a small one; it consists only of what touches his awareness. There is no war, no politics.

Does Parker himself change at all? It seems to me he mellows the slightest bit. Some of that may be Claire's doing, but some may simply be time. Parker's not much for small talk, and his humor is pretty much limited to irony, but I'd say he's somewhat better company in the later books.

Still, you wouldn't want to rile him.

I had the feeling, when I signed on to introduce these books, that the project would have me reading the books again. And I've been doing just that, and not only the three it's been my pleasure to introduce. When I took a moment to discuss opening lines, one of the books I picked up was *The Black Ice Score*. I read it through, and the two that followed it, *The Sour Lemon Score* and *Deadly Edge*. Next is *Slayground,* but I think I'll drop back first and refresh my memory of Parker's meeting with Claire, in *The Rare Coin Score.*

I remember when Don researched that one. I took him along to a numismatic convention in Indianapolis, where he enjoyed himself talking to coin dealer friends of mine. He used Indianapolis for the book's setting, used the hotel as well, changing its name from the Claypool to the Claymore.

What is it that makes the books so rereadable? They're suspenseful, but that is less a factor when you've already read them. They're brilliantly written, too, and it's nice watching a master at work, but I don't think that's enough to explain the phenomenon.

It's Parker, I guess, when all is said and done. He's a sociopath, I suppose, and God knows he's got the social skills of a boulder, but the choices he makes and the way he executes them make him compellingly interesting. Even when you know what he's going to do next, it's just plain fascinating to watch him do it.

And that's enough from me. Here's Parker in *Backflash*—and, whether you're reading it for the first time or the fifth, I've a feeling you're going to enjoy yourself.

Evidently Levi Stahl and Maggie Hivnor at University of Chicago Press decided I was the go-to guy for Westlake introductions. Five years after Don's death, Levi and Ethan Iverson went through Don's files, and Levi did a brilliant job of winnowing essays and introductions and correspondence, along with a rich chunk of a never-published memoir, into The Getaway Car, *a hearty compendium of the man's nonfiction. Could I supply an introduction? Of course I could:*

Sometime in the early spring of 1959 I plucked a book from a shelf in Yellow Springs, Ohio, and paid 35¢ for it. The title was *All My Lovers,* by Alan Marshall, and I bought it because I noted that it had been published by Midwood. Back in August I had sat up late in my parents' house in Buffalo, writing a book for Midwood, and

I'd since returned to Antioch College, where I was assiduously ne-
glecting my studies while writing a couple more books for the same
publisher, all of them examples of what we've since learned to call
Midcentury Erotica.

And now I'd actually found a Midwood title offered for sale. I
took it home and read it, and realized right away that Alan Marshall,
whoever he might be, was pretty good. I kept reading, and encountered a scene I still recall. A principal character was a cad who had,
in the manner of his tribe, behaved badly with a young woman from
el barrio. Her brothers responded by paying him a visit and beating
the crap out of him.

And then they left, and I'll quote the scene's closing words from
memory: "They did not take anything. They were not thieves."

Damn. This guy Marshall was good.

He was, as you've probably worked out on your own, Donald E.
Westlake, whom I was yet to meet. He, however, had already met
me, when I turned up in New York during Christmas vacation and
dropped in at the Scott Meredith office. That was where I had worked
from August 1957 to May 1958, and it was where Don was working
that December. I had a brief conversation with Henry Morrison, my
agent, and Don will share his recollection of the moment later in this
volume.

So he met me, but it was one-sided; his was just a face in the
background. Come summer, I'd finished the year at Antioch and tak-
en a room at the Hotel Rio on West 47th Street; I planned to spend
the summer writing more Midcentury Erotica before returning to
Yellow Springs for a final year.

(Shows what I knew. The school had other ideas, and while I was
at the Rio they sent me a letter, informing me that they felt I'd be
happier elsewhere. Boy, were they ever right.)

One of the Rio's charms (and they were thin on the ground) was
its proximity to the Scott Meredith offices, then at Fifth Avenue and
47th Street. I was a frequent visitor—to drop off a manuscript, to

sign a contract, to pick up a check—and at one such visit I met Don. The work day was ending, and we introduced ourselves, and he suggested we go get a beer.

Why not?

One beer led to another, and we wound up at the Westlake apartment on West 46th between Ninth and Tenth. That's a desirable address nowadays, which just shows what a difference half a century can make. Don was living there with his wife, Nedra, and their infant son, Sean. (Don was given to introducing Nedra as "the first Mrs. Westlake," which turned out to be unintentionally prophetic.)

I stayed for dinner, and we talked far into the night. As we were apt to do for the next fifty years.

On three occasions, back in the Midcentury Erotica days, we collaborated, and the resultant books (*A Girl Called Honey, So Willing,* and *Sin Hellcat*) were as much fun as I've ever had at a typewriter. They bore a joint byline ("by Sheldon Lord and Alan Marshall") and the first carried a dedication: "To Don Westlake and Larry Block," it read, "who introduced us."

Indeed.

Speaking of introductions—

Once, four or five years before Don's death, I spotted a hand-lettered sign on the wall over his desk. NO MORE INTRODUCTIONS, it proclaimed. That struck me as bizarre. Here was this wonderfully personable fellow, always a genial and eager host; what made him resolve at this late date to quit introducing his guests to one another?

What he meant, I soon learned, was that he'd resolved to stop responding favorably to requests that he write an introduction to someone's new collection, or a review of someone's book, or indeed any of the occasional pieces that one is constantly being invited to turn out.

Pieces, in fact, which make up a substantial portion of this present volume. Don enjoyed this sort of writing, and as you'll soon see he was superb at it, but what made him forswear the pursuit was the amount of time and energy it took. He had books to write, and that's where he wanted to focus his efforts.

Well, I get the point. I receive a fair number of similar requests myself—one such has me writing the words you're now reading—and it sometimes strikes me that I could put my time to more productive use. But, see, I wouldn't; I'd spend those hours playing computer solitaire, or posting inanities on Facebook, or hopscotching my way through Wikipedia.

So what the hell.

As for Don's labor in this varietal vineyard, I'm grateful for it; to it we owe this book's existence. I've read most of these pieces, but read them again as preparation for this foreword. (And that's another way introductions drain one's batteries. You don't just have to write 1000 words. First, you have to read fifty or a hundred times as many words of the material you've agreed to introduce. In this instance it was a pleasure. That, alas, is not always the case.)

It has been my delight to count as friends a couple of people who've never written a bad sentence, a clumsy paragraph, or a dull page. Evan Hunter was one. Donald E. Westlake was another.

Levi Stahl has done a superb job of sifting through Don's miscellaneous effort, separating the best of the wheat from the rest of the wheat—Don didn't do chaff—and organizing and notating the result. If I'm to take issue with anything, it's with a word he uses.

Jokes.

In his introduction, Levi describes these selections as being replete with jokes, and says Don found it almost impossible to write a page without putting in a joke. Now I read the entire book, and I can't recall a single joke.

A joke is something a comic tells. A joke generally starts with a guy walking into a bar. Or two guys, or even three.

This is a joke:

A Frenchman, a German, and a Jew walk into a bar.

The Frenchman says, "I am tired and thirsty. I must have wine!"

The German says, "I am tired and thirsty. I must have beer!"

The Jew says, "I am tired and thirsty. I must have diabetes."

There. That's a joke, and as far as I can tell, it's the only one you'll find in this book.

What you will find, however, and I suspect you'll find it on every page, is wit. Don was a wonderfully witty man, a fellow of infinite jest, and he took pains to make what he wrote amusing. Wit enlivened his conversation, even as it brightened his writing, fiction and nonfiction alike. In his fiction, his goal was to tell a story; in his other writing, he strove to relate an incident or convey information or make a point. In either case, it was second nature for him to do so with wit and humor.

The Getaway Car. It's an inspired title, and Abby's epigraph is dead accurate. While aspects of their author found their way into every one of his characters, when Don settled himself behind the wheel (and settled may not be *le mot juste* here) he became Stan Murch, ace wheelman of the Dortmunder gang. Like another of his characters, Don's ideal car was one that would get you from Point A to Point B in zero seconds.

When I met him, Don's New York State driver's license had been suspended; this happens when you've drawn enough speeding tickets, and he was always good at that. He wouldn't have wanted a car anyway on West 46th Street, but that changed when he moved out to Canarsie. And the day came when the three-year suspension was up, and his license was restored.

Whereupon he bought a car, and applied for insurance. And was astonished when the insurance company gave him a safe driver discount, because he hadn't had an accident or a speeding ticket in the past three years.

There's a word for that sort of thing. Westlakean.

An interviewer once asked John O'Hara if he missed the old days of the Algonquin Round Table.

"No," he said. "When Benchley died, the party was over."

I know what he meant.

Charles Willeford

Some years after Charles Willeford's death, I was asked to write an introduction for a paperback edition of his novel, The Shark-Infested Custard. *I'd reprint it here, but just about everything I said wound up in my* Mystery Scene *column, so for once I'll spare you the repetition.*

I had more to say and more room to say it in the column—though not quite enough room, as it turned out. Kate Stine had to do some judicious cutting for space reasons; being under no such constraints here, I'm able to publish it as written:

In the summer of 1985, Lynne and I moved from New York to Fort Myers Beach, Florida.

It's hard to remember why. We were both New Yorkers in a rather profound way, and we weren't likely to be happy anywhere else. We bought a big old house right on the Gulf, and the first morning I walked a few steps from my back door to the beach, turned right, and walked for a mile or so and back. The next morning I turned left instead of right, walked a mile, came back. By the third morning I was ready to go home.

After we'd been there a few months I got a phone call from Dennis McMillan, the small-press publisher. Dennis had been publishing the uncollected work of Fredric Brown, and had commissioned me to write an introduction for his edition of *The Case of the Dancing Sandwiches*, but that's not what he was calling about. He was in a car, he said, with Charles and Betsy Willeford, and he wasn't far from Fort Myers, and he thought they might stop by.

That sounded good to us. Our neighbors were pleasant enough, but we were starved for company down there, and I welcomed the opportunity to spend a little time with someone who was not only a writer but whose work I very much admired. I wasn't familiar with much of Willeford's early work, but I'd read his first Hoke Mosely novel, *Miami Blues*, shortly after its publication in 1984, and grabbed up the sequel, *New Hope for the Dead* as soon as it came my way.

Dennis showed up an hour or so after he called, with Charles and Betsy in tow, and the five of us sat around talking for a while and then went out for a meal. I don't remember where we went or what we ate, but I do recall two things about our conversation.

The first was that Charles talked at some length about a book he'd written and self-published eight years previously. It was called *A Guide for the Undehemorrhoided*, and it clearly concerned a subject about which Charles felt strongly; indeed, he'd written and published it as a service to his fellow man, recounting his own experience in an effort to disabuse the reader of the notion that surgery of this sort could possibly be a Good Idea.

"I'll send you a copy," he said.

He never did. It's not impossible that I showed a lack of enthusiasm at the prospect, and that this led him to drop the notion. It's also possible that it slipped his mind. So I never did have a look at the book—until a few minutes ago, when I Googled my way to Dennis's website, where I found the first few thousand words of the book. Here's how it begins:

> "In hospital language a patient does not urinate, micturate, pee, piss, or take a leak. He voids. Or, as in my case, he is unable to void.
>
> "Hospital jargon is mid-Victorian. My hemorrhoids were not chopped out, hacked away, or operated upon. Instead, my asshole was dilated and debrided. There is no sex talk in a hospital

either. Sex organs, male and female, when they are mentioned at all, are discussed formally, as elimination tools; nor is there, apparently, any distinction made between toilets for men and women. Whoever gets inside first has possession, and then there are no locks on the doors. If the doors were labeled, one suspects they would be called 'Necessary Rooms,' the euphemism for the toilets of our Gilded Age.

"Several years ago, before I ever thought of entering a hospital, a friend told me that a nurse's aide would give a man a slow handjob for five bucks. Unsurprised at the time, I filed the information away, thinking I might be able to use it in a novel some day. I have been sorry since that I failed to press my friend for details. On the disinterested outside, I had no reason to disbelieve him. But on the inside, watching these harried, grimly smiling nurse's aides—probably the lowest I.Q. occupational group of employees in the nation—rushing about inefficiently, but earning every cent of their $2.40 an hour, I wondered vaguely how my friend had gone about getting his slow handjob. He would have had to draw them a picture. However, discounting the denseness of the nurse's aides' understanding, the lack of privacy, the hospital stench and the permeating reek of indignant death—these factors in combination—drove all thoughts of and about sex from my mind during the two weeks of my stay."

I certainly wish I'd accepted Charles's offer with more enthusiasm, and in retrospect it's hard to imagine why I didn't. What did I think I'd get from Willeford? Something dry and clinical? Something impersonal?

Fat chance.

At some point during our lunch, Charles fixed an eye on me and began talking about people somewhere—Southeast Asia? Maybe—who ate cat. There was, he said, an informal society of men who had eaten cat, and they looked for and acknowledged one another. One man might look at another and say something along the lines of, "You eat cat, don't you?" And the other might smile and nod in acknowledgment, or raise an eyebrow.

I don't remember what I said to this. I didn't have a clue where he was going with this, and in my puzzlement I may have smiled, or raised an eyebrow. I don't think I nodded.

"Now you," Charles said, "you look to me like a man who has eaten cat."

Now at the time I was a vegetarian, so I hadn't eaten so much as a tuna fish sandwich for seven or eight years, never mind a pussycat. But all I did was say that I hadn't in fact ever eaten cat.

Charles seemed to find the admission disappointing. "I'm surprised," he said. "I thought you might well be a man who has eaten cat."

Thinking back, it strikes me that I might at this point have asked Charles if in fact *he* had ever eaten cat. Maybe he was waiting to be asked. But I didn't ask, nor did he volunteer any further information on the subject. Indeed, I think someone was kind enough to change the subject, and we went on to talk about something else—which, unlike the putative ingestion of cat, has left my memory altogether.

I wonder what he meant. Was there a sexual undertone to all of this, was "eating cat" a faintly veiled euphemism for cunnilingus? That occurred to me at the time, naturally enough, but I didn't think so then, nor do I think so now. I just did a Google search and learned more about the subject of human consumption of cat meat than I ever wanted to know, and my guess, after all these years, is that Charles found the topic interesting enough to toss it into the conversation, just to see what came back.

And did Charles ever eat cat? I suppose I should have asked him when I had the chance. But I didn't, and so I don't know, and don't need to know.

But I'll say this much. I wouldn't put it past him.

*　　　*　　　*

I saw Charles two or three times after that. Within a year of our initial meeting, I was invited to participate in the Miami Book Fair, where I appeared on a panel. I believe Charles had organized the panel, and suspect he was the source of my own invitation. He was in the audience, and we chatted before and after, but I don't remember what we talked about. Not cat, I'm fairly certain, as I would have remembered.

I encountered him again in Key West, where we both took part in a literary symposium in January, 1988. The topic was *Whodunit? The Art & Tradition of Mystery Literature,* and there were enough interesting writers participating to offset the academic tone set by the sponsors. I ran into Charles and Betsy several times in the course of the weekend, and again enjoyed their company. Sometimes I'd catch him eyeing me speculatively, as if wondering whether I'd ever eaten cat.

I do recall two conversations with Charles, though I can't say if they took place in Miami or Key West. Once he was recounting his experiences in the horse cavalry, when they'd been required to kill a dozen or so of their horses. Whoever was ordered to do the deed walked the length of a file of horses, shooting each of the beasts in the head in turn. What greatly impressed Charles was that the shooting of one horse made no apparent impression on the others. Each stood there stolidly until it was its turn, at which time it fell down dead.

On another occasion he spoke of the high proportion of clinical psychopaths one encountered in the military. There were, he announced, no end of men who liked being in the service because it gave them the opportunity to kill other men. They didn't seem to care whom they killed, or why, just so they got to do it.

I subsequently read his first-published memoir, *Something About a Soldier,* which came out in 1986, and it seems to me that he made some mention there of the psychopaths and the dead horses.

The Key West event was just about the last thing I did in Florida before taking leave of the state. Within a month Lynne and I had closed our house and took off for two years without a fixed address, driving back and forth across the country, stopping here and there for as little as a day or as much as a month, visiting every town and hamlet we could find named Buffalo (don't ask), getting to no end of national parks and roadside attractions, along with innumerable towns and hamlets not named Buffalo, all in an attempt to see as much of the country as we could while figuring out where we would like to live next. The answer to that last question was probably obvious all along, but it took us a while to nail it down, and finally on St. Patrick's Day of 1990 we returned to New York, and we've been here ever since.

Meanwhile, Charles Willeford had died—in Miami, on March 27, 1988. That was long before Google, long before email, long before I even thought about getting a computer, and no one could have called me with the news because it was long before cell phones, too, and I was in a motel somewhere—Buffalo Gap, Texas, maybe, or Buffalo Center, Iowa. So it was months before I learned he was gone, but I remember the feeling of loss and sadness. I'd known Charles was not in the best of health; he didn't talk about it, but it was evident. So in that sense the news was not unexpected. But it was shocking all the same; when one meets with so clear and distinct a voice, one expects it to be around forever.

Not long after Charles's death I began to hear the rumors. Charles had left a fifth Hoke Moseley novel, an impossibly dark novel, in which either Hoke killed his two daughters, or died himself, or both. And the book would eventually be published, or was deemed too dark to be published, or . . . well, various rumors advanced various possibilities.

This sort of rumor is not uncommon, both before and after the death of a popular writer, especially one with a beloved series character. Several years before John D. MacDonald died, fans were speculating about the likelihood of a final Travis McGee novel; each of the books had a color in the title (*The Deep Blue Goodbye, The Green Ripper, The Scarlet Ruse*), and the word was that this last book would have Black in the title, and McGee would die at the end of it. The rumors increased when John D. passed. Yes, he had indeed written such a book! Yes, it had Black in the title! Yes, McGee would die on the last page! Yes, it would be published!

Wrong, wrong, wrong, and wrong.

Once in an indigo moon, the rumor proves true. Agatha Christie wrote not one but two novels for posthumous publication, signing off on both Jane Marple and Hercule Poirot. (Both were written decades earlier.)

The Willeford rumor persisted, and it turned out to be partially true. The book was called *Grimhaven*, and one can find the following notation about it in the Willeford archive at the Broward County Library: *NOTE: as per Betsy Willeford: "Ms. of the 'black Hoke Moseley', never published, sold to a small but ruthless group of collectors in the form of Xerox copies. May not be copied in the library by patrons who'll wholesale it on the Internet."*

Five or six years after its author's death, someone sent me a photocopy of the manuscript of *Grimhaven*. I read it right away, and saw at once that it was not intended as a fifth Hoke Moseley book but as that series' second volume. It had been written as a sequel to *Miami Blues*, a sequel Willeford did not at all want to write.

Miami Blues, which introduced Hoke Moseley, was the first book of Willeford's to get a strong promotional effort, and it profited immensely by it. The book got a very strong and favorable response from the critics, drew a lot of attention to its author, and sold well. The publisher, not too surprisingly, wanted Willeford to write a sequel, and indeed to make Hoke a series character.

Should it surprise us to learn that Charles Willeford, whose characters constantly exhibit quirky, contrary, self-defeating behavior, should balk at the notion? He really didn't want to write another Hoke Moseley book, and his publisher really wanted him to write that and nothing else.

So Charles sat down and knocked out a book designed to nip the series in the bud. In all likelihood his publishers would pass on the book, but if they went ahead and brought it out, well, the series would at the very least end with the second volume. Because in its pages Hoke, this wonderfully interesting and sympathetic hero, murders his daughters, gets arrested for the crime, and looks forward to being confined to a prison cell for the rest of his life, thus fulfilling the book's epigraph quote, from Blaise Pascal: "All human evil comes from a single cause, man's inability to sit still in a room by himself." Hoke is destined to do just that, in a small room indeed, and the likelihood of our reading further about him would seem remote at best.

Do you think I should have prefaced this with a spoiler alert? Well, too bad. The spoiler's intentional, because I'd prefer to discourage you from seeking out and reading the manuscript. Betsy Willeford would rather you didn't, and I'm with her on this one. And, let me assure you, it's not a very good book. But then it wasn't really trying to be.

I wasn't privy to the conversations and correspondence that followed the submission of *Grimhaven*, but I can imagine, and so I suspect can you. The publisher had his way, and *Grimhaven* went back on the shelf, and soon enough Charles had produced an eminently successful sequel to *Miami Blues*, with the magnificent title of *New Hope for the Dead*. (That comes from an old joke, incidentally, in which it's cited as the ultimate Reader's Digest essay.) I say "soon enough" because the second book appeared in 1985, a year after the first. *Sideswipe* came out two years later, with *The Way We Die Now* following in the year of Willeford's death.

Charles Willeford took writing very seriously, and applied himself to it wholeheartedly for some forty years. He started out as a poet; his first book, *Proletarian Laughter*, was a collection of poems. He began publishing paperback fiction while serving his second hitch in the military, and kept at it, and worked hard at it.

With the Hoke Moseley novels, he got a taste of the commercial success that had for so long eluded him. When I learned of his death, I was struck by the irony of it; he was just beginning to get somewhere, and the Fates took him out of the game.

Later, when I learned about and read *Grimhaven*, and realized how hard Charles had worked to keep success at bay, I saw the irony to be vaster than I'd guessed. You could even call it Willefordian.

Not long ago I finally got around to reading *I Was Looking For a Street*, Willeford's second volume of memoir. (It was published in 1988, two years after *Something About a Soldier*, but covers an earlier period in its author's life.) It made it very clear to me how the man was able consistently to create wildly idiosyncratic characters. He came by it honestly; their quirks were his.

The hero of *Cockfighter*, resolutely mute throughout the book's pages because of an oath he'd made to himself. The cheerful old man in *Sideswipe*, taking his daily constitutional walk through his suburban neighborhood, meeting and greeting his neighbors, even as he sets about poisoning all their dogs. And Hoke Moseley, for heaven's sake, quirky enough even before he decided to strangle his beloved daughters. Nobody else ever came up with characters like that, and I don't know that anybody ever could.

Their origins become clear—well, clearer, anyway—when you read *I Was Looking For a Street*. It never seems to have occurred to Willeford to be embarrassed about anything, or about sharing anything with the reader. One gets a hint of this in the passage I quoted from the hemorrhoid book, and it's evident throughout the memoir.

(This lack of embarrassment, I should note, extended to his early career as a writer. His books for years were published by third-rate soft porn houses like Beacon. Now I wrote for Beacon, and so did any number of writers I've known, but none of us used our own names on those books. I'm sure Charles knew that Beacon was not on the same level with, say, Alfred Knopf, but they were his books and he put his name on them. He didn't mind seeing them republished years later in hardcover, either. Does this mean that he took them seriously? Or just that he took them no less seriously than he took anything else?)

*   *   *

Then too, there's the remarkably matter-of-fact manner in which various phenomena are reported. At one work camp where young Charles stayed, he talks of one barnyard chore that the older boys found particularly desirable—because it gave them the chance to fuck the calves. He just says this in passing and goes right on to something else.

He develops a friendship with another teenage hobo, whose main goal in life is to get a real cowboy hat, a Stetson; once he has one, he'll feel he's ready to quit the road and go home. Charles vows privately that he'll get such a hat for his friend, and indeed the day comes when he sees the perfect hat on a peg in some bar or restaurant. He grabs it up and wears it out of there, and the hat feels just about perfect on his own head, and he wants that hat as he's never wanted anything in his life.

But he promised it to his friend—even though the friend knows nothing of the promise. So Charles feels himself honor-bound to give the hat to his friend, because that's the right thing to do, and it would be wrong to keep it.

The moral imperative of bestowing the hat upon his friend, combined with the clear immorality of stealing it from its rightful owner—I'll tell you, if I came across that in a novel, I'd know right away who wrote it.

It was at the end of the memoir that I found what seems to me to be the key to Charles Willeford and his work. He supplies a sort of coda to the work, a poem in which he takes to task his absent father and blames him for making him grow up a sociopath.

Willeford a sociopath? Really?

To be sure, literary ability is no guarantee against a sociopathic personality, as Norman Mailer found out to his chagrin after he'd championed Jack Henry Abbott. But does a sociopath ever recognize himself as such?

And can a self-diagnosed sociopath be at the same time an intensely moral person? Can one be a sociopath, virtually unaware of socially prescribed morality, and yet be consumed with the desire to do the right thing?

That strikes me as a spot-on description of just about every character Willeford ever wrote. How could he come up with characters like that? My God, how could he help it?

I haven't reread any of Willeford's work since I came upon that revelation in *I Was Looking For a Street*. I intend to. I think it will illuminate the work, and that the work will shed a little more light on the man himself. I'm grateful that I knew him, however briefly and superficially. I wish I could have known him better, and longer.

And in Conclusion . . .

One writer whose work I read when I was getting started, and whom I met toward the end of his own long life, was William Campbell Gault. He started out writing stories for the pulp magazines, then moved to crime novels when the pulps disappeared. When his sales slumped, he switched to juvenile sports fiction, of which science fiction critic Damon Knight wrote, "I liked the characterization in those stories; I liked the description; I liked the fist fights; I liked the love interest. I like everything about them, except what they were all about."

For twenty years Bill Gault wrote sports stories, and then he went back to crime and picked up his series detective, Brock Callahan, and resumed writing about him. He'd won an Edgar in 1952 for his first mystery, added a Shamus in 1983, and finished up with a couple of Lifetime Achievement awards by the time he died in 1995 at the age of 85.

One thing he wrote sticks in my mind. I'm not sure where or when I read it, probably *Writers Digest*, certainly well over fifty years ago. It went something like this: "When I set out to be a writer, I wanted to give Ernest Hemingway a run for his money. But it didn't take me too long to find out I couldn't hope to be better than a third- or fourth-rate Hemingway. So I quit trying, and what I found out was I could be a pretty good William Campbell Gault."

That's quoted from memory, but it's not too far removed from another observation Gault made at a later date: "I'm proud of what I can do in my field. And I'm proud of the field. I don't need any false additions to that. If I could write like John Cheever, I'd write like Cheever. Unfortunately I can't, so I write as well as I can and as fast as I can. And some of it is good."

I've a feeling many crime writers could say something similar.

For my part, I'm grateful to have spent a lifetime shaded by the broad canopy of crime fiction. I've never felt limited by the genre, as it has room within its confines for everything from Lillian Jackson Braun's cat mysteries to Raskolnikov and Hamlet. And I've felt nourished throughout by my colleagues and my readers.

(My friend Sparkle Hayter, when asked what sort of people tend to read her books, has said that the only common denominator she's noted is that her readers are significantly brighter and better-looking than average. Curiously enough, I've noticed the same thing about my own readers.)

And I hope that'll do for a summing-up.

About the Author

Lawrence Block has been writing award-winning mystery and suspense fiction for half a century. His most recent novels are *The Burglar Who Counted the Spoons*, featuring Bernie Rhodenbarr; *Hit Me,* featuring Keller; and *A Drop of the Hard Stuff,* featuring Matthew Scudder, played by Liam Neeson in the film, *A Walk Among the Tombstones*. Several of his other books have been filmed, although not terribly well. He's well known for his books for writers, including the classic *Telling Lies for Fun & Profit,* and *The Liar's Bible*. In addition to prose works, he has written episodic television (*Tilt!*) and the Wong Kar-wai film, *My Blueberry Nights*. He is a modest and humble fellow, although you would never guess as much from this biographical note.

Email: lawbloc@gmail.com
Twitter: @LawrenceBlock
Facebook: lawrence.block
Website: lawrenceblock.com